Thomas Erskine

and Trial by Jury

John Hostettler

Thomas Erksine
and Trial by Jury
John Hostettler

ISBN 9781904380 597 (Paperback)
ISBN 9781906534 868 (e-book)

Published 2010 by
Waterside Press Ltd.
Sherfield Gables
Sherfield on Loddon
Hook
Hampshire
United Kingdon RG27 0JG

Previous publication
This work was originally published
in hardback by Barry Rose in 1996.
Waterside Press are grateful to the family
of Barry Rose for allowing the work to be
reproduced here in its original form.

Telephone
+44(0)1256 882250
Low cost UK landline calls
0845 2300 733
E-mail
enquiries@watersidepress.co.uk
Online catalogue
WatersidePress.co.uk

Cataloguing-In-Publication Data
A catalogue record for this book can be
obtained on request from the British
Library.

Cover design
© 2010 Waterside Press. Cover features
original coins minted in celebration of
famous trials involving Thomas Erskine.

UK distributor
Gardners Books, 1 Whittle Drive, East-
bourne, East Sussex, BN23 6QH.
Tel: +44 (0)1323 521777;
sales@gardners.com; www.gardners.com

North American distributor
International Specialised Book Services
(ISBS), 920 NE 58th Ave, Suite 300, Port-
land, Oregon, 97213, USA.
Tel: 1 800 944 6190 Fax: 1 503 280 8832;
orders@isbs.com; www.isbs.com

Printed by
Good News Press, Ongar

e-book
Thomas Erskine and Trial by Jury is
available as an ebook (e-book ISBN
9781906534868) and also to subscribers
of Myilibrary and Dawsonera.

Thomas Erskine
and Trial by Jury

John Hostettler

❄ WATERSIDE PRESS

Also by John Hostettler

A History of Criminal Justice in England and Wales

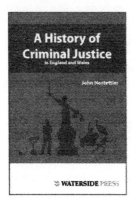

An ideal introduction, charting all the main developments of criminal justice, from Anglo-Saxon dooms to the Common Law, struggles for political, legislative and judicial ascendency and the formation of the modern-day Criminal Justice System. 'Every student entering law school should have a copy and read it': *Criminal Law and Justice Weekly*

Jan 2009 | 352 pp | Paperback ISBN 9781904380511
Ebook ISBN 9781906534790

Sir William Garrow

His Life, Times and Fight for Justice
Co-author **Richard Braby**
Foreword **Geoffrey Robertson QC**

The 'Lost Story of William Garrow' formed the basis for the successful BBCI TV prime-time drama series 'Garrow's Law'. This book tells the real story behind the drama: of Garrow's life, upbringing and fight with the legal establishment to change the face of the English criminal trial. 'A blockbuster of a book': **Phillip Taylor MBE**, barrister.

Jan 2010 | 272 pp | 1st Ed. | Hardback ISBN 9781904380559 | Ebook ISBN 9781906534820

More titles and full details at WatersidePress.co.uk

Contents

We are servants of the law in order that we may be free.
Cicero. *Pro Cluentio*. 53,146.

About the author

John Hostettler was a practising solicitor in London for 35 years as well as undertaking political and civil liberties cases in Nigeria, Germany and Aden. He sat as a magistrate for a number of years and has also been a chairman of tribunals. He played a leading role in the abolition of flogging in British colonial prisons and served on a Home Office Committee to revise the rules governing electoral law in Britain. He holds several university degrees and three doctorates.

His other biographical works include those on Thomas Wakley, Sir James Fitzjames Stephen, Sir Edward Carson, Sir Edward Coke, Lord Halsbury and Sir Matthew Hale. His books for Waterside Press include *The Criminal Jury Old and New: Jury Power from Early Times to the Present Day*; *Fighting for Justice: The History and Origins of Adversary Trial*; *Hanging in the Balance: A History of the Abolition of Capital Punishment in Britain* (with Dr Brian P. Block); *A History of Criminal Justice in England and Wales*; and most recently, *Sir William Garrow: His Life, Times and Fight for Justice*.

Barry Rose

Barry Rose published this book in hardback in 1996. I had first met Barry in Chichester on the occasion of his publishing my first book four years earlier. We were to go to lunch (or luncheon as he always called it) together and he was waiting for me at the door to his offices. My first impression was of Mr. Pickwick and that was to last over the many years I knew him and became his friend. At the time Barry was publishing a number of journals and his pride and joy was the *Justice of the Peace*, the oldest legal journal in the world having been published weekly continuously since 1837. He was its editor-in-chief and often wrote the weekly tongue in cheek column signed Brougham which was the first part of the journal I turned to each week when I was a sitting magistrate.

Barry had a love of the law and was always keen to meet interesting people in the legal world. He had a deep interest in, and knowledge of, the law and its practitioners and enjoyed his frequent visits to legal London around Lincoln's Inn, the High Court and places with a Dickensian aura such as the Temple and Chancery Lane. He thoroughly relished partaking of good food and drink and enjoying the company with him. There was usually some legal talk accompanied by much wit over a meal. All manner of staff knew him affectionately as 'Mr. Rose' at places such as The Garrick Club, Atheneum and Simpson's-in-the-Strand and his occasional receptions at these and other places were legendary affairs.

He could be distinguished by his sartorial preferences. He wore a monocle and deplored my use of spectacles for reading. Ever with a buttonhole and often sporting a bow tie he wore to work a dark suit with a waistcoat. To top it all was his famous billycock hat. On one occasion when we were walking from his office to his favourite restaurant in Chichester, the "Little London", he remarked to me that I was not properly dressed. As I was also wearing a dark suit and a tie I asked in what way? He replied that I was not wearing a waistcoat. I soon took the opportunity to buy a rather colourful waistcoat which I then always wore when in his company.

Barry was a very kind person who found it very difficult to turn down a manuscript submitted to him for possible publication. Unlike most, if not all, modern publishers he would read manuscripts even if badly typed or written by hand. He often did this on the train, where there were no telephones and few interruptions until the advent of the mobile phone, when travelling to and from London.

Widely known as the "Gentleman Publisher", Barry died on 19 July 2005, two days after his 84th birthday. At his funeral at Chichester Crematorium the mourners were so many that provision had to be made to relay the service to those outside who could not gain admittance to the chapel. As was said on that occasion "He Lived Life to Entertain and be Entertained". He is deeply missed but his work lives on.

John Hostettler
March 2010

Thomas Erskine and William Garrow: A Note

Now that the lost story of Sir William Garrow's role in changing the face of the common law criminal trial has been brought before the general public[1], it is instructive to re-consider the unique career of Thomas Erskine. The issue as a paperback of this book that first appeared in 1996 should fill the bill. Very little other writing on Erskine is extant.

Garrow and Erskine were contemporaries who often appeared in court in the same case – sometimes in harness and sometimes on opposite sides. There is evidence that they were friends. Both rose from rags to riches, earning huge fees and, more importantly, by sheer skill and eloquence they came to be regarded as two of the brightest stars ever to shine in English criminal law. Unlike another brilliant lawyer, Henry Brougham, who had a superior manner before juries and was rarely successful with them, it was perhaps because of their relatively lowly start in life that Garrow and Erskine both proved able to empathise with juries and somehow infuse their ideas into the minds of those twelve good men and true before whom they so frequently appeared. In court Erskine stood thin and erect, had a clear and melodic voice and a penetrating eye, but Garrow's questioning of hostile witnesses was more inventive.

Both also undertook civil cases with great success. In what became known as *The Case of Mrs Day's Baby* (involving inheritance) Garrow scored over Erskine to the latter's chagrin but, on the other side of the account, is the astonishing case where, in sparkling form, Erskine persuaded a jury that his client who was guilty of adultery should be awarded heavy damages although the client was the guilty party. Only the intervention of the judge who required the jury to reconsider its verdict prevented a miscarriage of justice. Both these cases are cited in this book.

Garrow made his name, and introduced human rights into the criminal law, in the sordid atmosphere of the Old Bailey. Erskine too appeared at "The Bailey" and shone in the state trials that rocked England (and Scotland)

---

1. See *Sir William Garrow: His Life Times and Fight for Justice* (2010), Hostettler J and Braby R, Waterside Press.

when the government of William Pitt took fright at the French Revolution. His greatest claim, to fame came with his defence, without fee, of the prisoners in the great treason trials of 1794 that threatened to destroy the Rule of Law. Habeas Corpus had been suspended, the Old Bailey was surrounded by troops, and a Special Powers Act was mooted to deal with an imaginary revolutionary plot. No less than 800 warrants were prepared to arrest people who were merely calling for franchise reform but charged with "compassing the death of the king", in what historians call "The English Terror". There was an open presumption of guilt and, with their lives at risk, Edmund Burke accused them of being assassins and urged that the disease of the body politic demanded the "critical terrors of the cautery and the knife".

In unprecedented scenes in court, with a special commission of six judges, Erskine wooed the jury and decisively turned the first three trials against the government. Each of the prisoners was found not guilty. Erskine was feted by the huge crowds massed outside the court in every direction. The remaining warrants were consigned to the rubbish bin and England's freedom was saved. Lord John Russell wrote that "Defended by [Erskine], the government found in the meanest individual whom they attacked, the tongue of Cicero and the soul of Hampden, an invincible orator, and an undaunted patriot."

Many of Erskine's speeches reveal great eloquence, skill and courage and like, Garrow, he changed the course of criminal history, not least when he destroyed the hateful doctrine of constructive treason by his successful defence of Lord George Gordon following the great destruction in London of the "no popery" riots of 1780. Erskine also introduced the "cab rank rule" at the Bar when he declared that, however much a prisoner might be regarded as guilty before his trial, he had the right to an advocate of his choice and that no advocate should decline to represent him but should act as counsel not as judge and jury. He took this stand when he appeared for Tom Paine, author of the *Rights of Man*, even though warned off and told it would cost him his position as legal adviser to the Prince of Wales, as indeed it did.

Garrow's impact in securing adversary trial had repercussions throughout the globe which are still with us today. And to his friend and colleague, Thomas Erskine, First Baron Erskine, goes the accolade of being the most outstanding advocate and champion of justice and liberty in English legal history.

Prologue

Liberty Safeguarded

Reign of Terror

The date was November 5, 1794. A verdict was awaited in the trial of Thomas Hardy—a shoemaker charged with high treason in "compassing the death of the King". Habeas corpus had been summarily suspended. The Old Bailey was surrounded by barriers and troops to keep out the press of anxious people thronging the streets. From mouth to mouth passed the word of the date. A fateful day for England.

On this day in 1604, Parliament had been in danger from Guy Fawkes and the Gunpowder Plot. On this day in 1688, William of Orange had landed at the small fishing village of Brixham to restore the liberties of England and the Protestant religion. Now, in 1794, these liberties were again in peril.

The eminent historian, J.R. Green, described the government's excesses in prosecution and attacks on freedom at the time as the "English Terror".[1] In similar vein Lord John Campbell called the frenzied attempts at repression, "a Reign of Terror".[2] Fortunately, the widespread coercion was halted in a series of explosive and historic State Trials by the singular skills and resolution of Thomas Erskine—England's foremost advocate.

---

1. *A Short History of the English People.* 818. 1874.
2. *Lives of the Chancellors.* vi. 460. 1847.

Portrait of Thomas Erskine, 1st Baron Erskine
by Sir William Charles Ross (1823)
© National Portrait Gallery, London

CHAPTER 1

Enlightenment

Humanity

Thomas Erskine was born into a fast-changing world on January 10, 1750. It was a time when the flame of the Enlightenment burned brightly throughout Europe. In Scotland, where Erskine was born, its glow centred on Edinburgh where Adam Smith and David Hume were busy destroying established beliefs with challenging new ideas on economics, religion and humanity.

The primary theme of the Enlightenment was that culture, in all its manifestations, embraces true knowledge which right reasoning can discover, leading mankind to happiness. Individuals are essentially equal and "man of reason and nature" is noble. All that is needed is intellectual freedom. Liberty would ensure progress.

This philosophy captured the minds of young Scottish intellectuals of whom Henry Brougham, afterwards to become Lord Chancellor, is a brilliant case in point. When he enrolled in the ancient University of Edinburgh in 1791 at the age of 13 Brougham was fired with an

1

enthusiasm to acquire every kind of knowledge. And where better when Edinburgh then had a higher intellectual repute than Oxford and Cambridge.

He chose to read humanity and philosophy which included mathematics, natural philosophy, ancient languages, political economy, rhetoric, logic, astronomy and moral philosophy. Incredibly, on many of these he was soon writing for the influential and at times irreverent *Edinburgh Review*, which he helped found, and which was sparking violent reactions in Scotland and England alike.

So far as law is concerned, it is little wonder that at this time Scotland brought forth the great titans of advocacy, Thomas Erskine, Henry Brougham and John Campbell. They did not all absorb the classical learning of Greece and Rome but they exemplified its spirit in the new age of Western thought. And, although they were sons of the Scottish Enlightenment, they came to believe that adequate scope for their talents lay only in London which drew them like a magnet with the prestige of its common law tradition and unique Inns of Court. The prizes of an English career cast a profound spell over them. The additional incentive was London's lively intellectual and social life.

When Thomas Erskine came to settle in London as a barrister, he soon excited wonder and awe at all levels of society. At a time of repression, induced by Pitt's fear of the spreading tentacles of the French Revolution, Erskine rose as if from nowhere to defend the liberties of Englishmen.

Many of his speeches to juries continue to burn as glowing lanterns in the literature of freedom. As with all who practise in the courts, no doubt his triumphs would have been fleeting but for the quality of those speeches· which have ensured to his victories a defiance of time.

Arguably, he still remains the brightest star of which the English Bar can boast.

Ideals of Law

It was a remarkable age. Montesquieu sowed the seeds of the new philosophy with his influential *De l'esprit des lois* (The Spirit of Laws) in the then novel and imaginative belief that the purpose of the criminal law should be to safeguard the liberty and security of the individual; that it should limit the power of the state in order to prevent despotism and arbitrary rule; and that its punishments should always be moderate.

It was a time when an Italian nobleman, Count Cesare Beccaria, was to secure an end to penal torture in many countries of Europe with his eloquent plea for humanity in the law in his *Dei Delitti e delle Pene* (Of Crimes and Punishments). Both Montesquieu and Beccaria expressed in the legal arena the ideals and aspirations of the Enlightenment and Beccaria acknowledged his debt to the older Montesquieu in his book when he wrote that he was following "the luminous footsteps of this great man".

It was a time that saw the publication of Adam Smith's *Wealth of Nations*, which transformed economic theory and practice, and David Hume's *Enquiry Concerning Human Understanding*, which brought new insights into civic morality. Both contributed to the Scottish Enlightenment and Adam Smith also acknowledged the inspiration of Montesquieu. It was an exciting age in which to enter the world.

CHAPTER 2

Early Years

Born to Poverty

On the face of it the young Erskine was born with a silver spoon in his mouth as a son of the 10th Earl of Buchan whose family had enjoyed a long connexion with Scottish royalty. However, the reality was different. Not only was he the youngest of three sons but the Earl had been reduced to poverty and moved his home from the ancestral castle to rooms in the Old Town of Edinburgh. It was there that Thomas was born, in the upper flat of a tall house at the head of Gray's Close.

The Old Town, consisting of houses built for medieval burghers, rises to great heights upon the narrow spine of rock between Edinburgh Castle and Holyrood Abbey. Several of the old dwellings, including that of John Knox, have painted timber ceilings profusely decorated with foliage, biblical scenes and mythical motifs. These lofty houses, with their narrow frontages and even narrower gaps between them, can still be seen today and together form a heritage treasure.

But in 1750 they were overcrowded, ill-furnished,

insanitary and broken up into small tenements. Even one of these, however, was to prove too expensive for the Earl and before long he was obliged to move his family to St Andrews, Fife, where he could live more cheaply.

Thomas, who as a youngster was quick, idle and frolicsome, was at first educated by his talented mother, Agnes Steuart, who possessed a powerful and cultivated intellect. Later, he was sent to school in the Old Town but returned home for his meals which consisted of porridge for breakfast and soup for dinner. When the family moved to Fife he became a pupil at St Andrews Grammar School.

Sailor

Public school and university were financially out of the question although for a few months Thomas managed to attend some classes at Edinburgh University. But he did move among circles which included peers, lawyers and government ministers and this provided an invaluable education in itself. On leaving school he wished to enter a profession but again his parents could not afford the expense involved.

In consequence, at the age of 14 he went to sea as a midshipman. He did so reluctantly since he now fancied a career in the army but the money required to buy a commission was not available. Whilst he was still hoping he would not have to become a sailor he explained why in a letter to his aunt. If he did, he wrote, he would not have the same opportunity to improve his learning as he would have at places where he would be stationed if he were a soldier.

I assure you, he continued, I could by no means put up without improving myself in my studies, for I can be

happy as the day is long with them, and would 10
times rather be at St Andrews, attending the classes
there, and even those I was at last year, viz. Natural
Philosophy and Mathematics (both of which I am
extremely fond of), than at the most beautiful place in
the world, with all manner of diversions, and
amusements.[1]

Of course, it may be that the young boy was writing what
he thought his aunt would want to hear but it reads like
a genuine desire for the intellectual development which
would be natural in one of his background.

Once in the navy, he wore the traditional blue jacket,
cocked hat and sword and served for four years in the
Tartar, a man-of-war commanded by the experienced sea
captain, Sir David Lindsay. He sailed mainly in the
Caribbean and off the coast of America. At one point, in
1765, he was struck by lightning in a storm but
fortunately suffered no lasting injuries. His appetite for
knowledge did not leave him, however, and he picked up
books in the ports he visited and did his best to take part
in and understand the indigenous local life.

In the West Indies, for instance, he joined in the dances
of the native people and from Kingston in Jamaica wrote
to his brother Henry: "The longer I stay in the West
Indies I find the country more healthful and the climate
more agreeable ... I am studying botany with Dr Butt, so
I will bring home drawings of all the curious plants, etc.,
and every thing that I see. I have sent Mamma home a
land turtle, to walk about Walcot garden; it is very pretty,
particularly its back, which is all divided into square

---

1.   Lord John Campbell. *Op.cit.*, 372.

lozenges, and the shell is as hard as a coat of mail".[2]

When Erskine was 18, his father died at Bath and was succeeded as Earl by his eldest son, David Steuart. Although having no inheritance from his father Thomas now left the navy, where he had become acting lieutenant, in accordance with his own desire and the wish of his mother. He could now afford to join the army and did so as an ensign in the Royals, or 1st Regiment of Foot. At first he was quartered in various provincial towns and in one of these he fell in love with Frances Moore, the daughter of the Member of Parliament for Marlow. On April 21, 1770, he married her, despite some opposition from his family. It was to prove a lasting and happy marriage.

On Erskine's regiment subsequently being sent to garrison Minorca, his wife accompanied him. They stayed on the island for two years and there he undertook a course in English literature and discovered the delights of Milton, Shakespeare, Dryden and Pope, from all of whose works he could recite long pieces from memory.

Cordial Brush with Dr Johnson

When Erskine returned to England on leave for six months he was introduced to London society by his wealthy relations. With his aristocratic lineage and charm of manner he was soon received in the distinguished patrician and literary circles of the town. James Boswell, in his *Life of Johnson,*[3] records that on April 6, 1772 he (Boswell) dined with the Doctor at Sir Alexander

---

2.   *Ibid.*, 375.
3.   1961 edn., 480.

Macdonald's, "where was a young officer in the
regimentals of the Scots Royal, who talked with a
vivacity, fluency, and precision so uncommon, that he
attracted particular attention. He proved to be the
Honourable Thomas Erskine, youngest brother to the Earl
of Buchan, who has since risen into such brilliant
reputation at the Bar in Westminster-hall".

Boswell then reveals the youthful Erskine as already
willing to join in the fray with the redoubtable Doctor:

> Fielding being mentioned, Johnson exclaimed, "he was
> a blockhead"; and upon my mentioning my
> astonishment at so strange an assertion, he said,
> "What I mean by his being a blockhead is that he was
> a barren rascal".
>
> *Boswell.* Will you not allow, Sir, that he draws very
> natural pictures of human life?
>
> *Johnson.* Why, Sir, it is of very low life. Richardson
> used to say, that had he not known who Fielding was,
> he should have believed he was an ostler. Sir, there is
> more knowledge of the heart in one letter of
> Richardson's than in all *Tom Jones.* I, indeed, never
> read *Joseph Andrews.*
>
> *Erskine.* Surely, Sir, Richardson is very tedious.
>
> *Johnson.* Why, Sir, if you were to read Richardson
> for the story, your impatience would be so much fretted
> that you would hang yourself. But you must read him
> for the sentiment, and consider the story as only giving
> occasion to the sentiment.

Full of himself, as he already was, Erskine told the
company that when he was in Minorca he had not only
read prayers, but preached two sermons to the regiment.
He then seemed to question the passage in scripture
where it is told that the angel of the Lord smote in one

night 40,000 Assyrians.

"Sir", responded Johnson, "you should recollect that there was a supernatural interposition; they were destroyed by pestilence. You are not to suppose that the angel of the Lord went about and stabbed each of them with a dagger, or knocked them on the head, man by man".[4]

Abuses in the Army

Later that year, despite, or perhaps because of, his low rank Erskine proclaimed himself a crusader against abuses in the army. He wrote, and arranged to have published, a bold and eloquent pamphlet with the title: "Observations on the Prevailing Abuses in the British Army, arising from the Corruption of Civil Government". To which he added, "A Proposal to the Officers towards obtaining an Addition to their pay".

In spite of this sweetener, and an assurance to the officers whom he desired to join with him to end the abuses that they would not be punished for mutiny, he published the pamphlet anonymously. Nevertheless, his authorship was an open secret and the pamphlet was widely circulated. Even at this early stage it was described by Jeremy Bentham as, "characterized by something different from common writing".[5]

Erskine's purpose was to rouse officers to a spirited and heretical, but as he saw it constitutional, demand that soldiers be able to enjoy the rights of useful citizens.

---

4.   *Ibid.*
5.   *Works.* x. 564. 1843.

At first view, he declared, this may appear to be a dangerous subject, and highly incompatible with the arbitrary principles of military government. What is termed remonstrance in a citizen, is supposed to be mutiny in a soldier; but mutiny I apprehend to be confined to the breach of discipline and subordination in an inferior to a superior in military command; soldiers do not give up their general rights as members of a free community; they are amenable to civil and municipal laws, as well as to their own martial code, and are therefore entitled to all the privileges with which a free form of government invests every individual; nay, it is to their virtue that all other parts of the community must ultimately trust for the enjoyment of their peaceable privileges; for, as Mr Pitt in his strong figurative eloquence expressed himself in Parliament, "To the virtue of the army we have hitherto trusted; to that virtue small as the army is, we must still trust and without that virtue the Lords, the Commons, and the people of England may entrench themselves behind parchment up to the teeth, but the sword will find a passage to the vitals of the Constitution".

Here we can discern the genesis of the advocate of the future. And he was to be encouraged by the knowledge that when the American War of Independence revealed deficiencies in the British army it adopted and benefited considerably from some of the reforms he had proposed.

Call of the Bar

In April 1773 Erskine was appointed lieutenant in his regiment. However, further promotion seemed distant since there was no reasonable prospect of purchasing a higher commission. Moreover, he no longer found barrack-room life congenial with a wife and family to look after.

The future looked bleak, therefore, when one day by chance he wandered into a courtroom of the Assizes in the town where he was stationed, still wearing his uniform. Lord Mansfield, whom Bentham once called his "living idol"[6] was the presiding Judge and he asked who the young soldier was. On learning that he was the youngest son of the late Earl of Buchan, and had sailed under his own nephew, Sir David Lindsay, he invited Erskine to sit with him on the Bench - a not uncommon practice at the time.

Mansfield explained to him the case which was being tried. But he was not responsible for Erskine, with a conceit already formed, thinking that he could do at least as well as the eloquent leaders of the circuit before him. This led him to resolve, there and then, to study law and become a barrister. That evening Mansfield invited the young man to dinner where Erskine told him of his plans. The astute Judge did not discourage him but advised him to consult his family first. When he did so his brothers said nothing to dissuade him and his mother was enthusiastic. Since he did not need to write to his wife we know nothing of her views.

Erskine thereupon decided to sell his commission to provide some finance in order to leave the army for the law. He joined Lincoln's Inn as a student on April 26, 1775, paying an enrolment fee of £3.3.4d. However, he was required to remain a student for five years unless he obtained a degree at Oxford or Cambridge, when the period would be reduced to three years. In the light of his

---

6.   *Works.* i. 247.

poverty this was the course he decided to follow.

Degree at Cambridge

Accordingly, he became a gentleman commoner of Trinity College, Cambridge on January 13, 1776, with the privilege of wearing a hat. As the son of a nobleman he was entitled to a degree without examination and, although he took rooms in the college, he did not study seriously or aspire to become a classical scholar in the University tradition. He did, however, practise English composition in verse and prose. And, in a portent of what was to come, he gained the prize in English Declamation for an oration on the "Glorious Revolution" of 1688 which was later published. More to his sense of fun, on the other hand, was his "To the College Barber", a burlesque parody of Gray's Ode, "Ruin seize thee ruthless King".

Interestingly, in his defence of Tom Paine in 1792 Erskine referred to the prize in the following manner:

> I was formerly called upon, under the discipline of a college, to maintain these truths, and was rewarded for being thought to have successfully maintained that our present Constitution was by no means a remnant of Saxon liberty, nor any other institution of liberty, but the pure consequence of the oppression of the Norman tenures, which, spreading the spirit of freedom from one end of the Kingdom to the other, enabled our brave fathers not to reconquer, but for the first time to obtain those privileges which are the inalienable inheritance of all mankind.[7]

---

7.   Howell's *State Trials*. xxii. 418. 1817.

With Paine he believed that English liberty was won from the usurped power of the Normans by struggles of the people.

At this time there was no Union debating society at Cambridge but Erskine took part in the debates at the *Robin Hood* in Coachmakers' Hall, London, to improve his fluency. Here, those attending, who included Members of Parliament, paid an entrance fee of 6d and received a glass of porter or punch which was said to have enhanced the display of oratory.

Whilst keeping his terms at Lincoln's Inn, and still at Cambridge, Erskine also studied law as a pupil in the chambers of Francis Buller, later an eminent Judge, and afterwards in those of George Wood, later Baron of the Exchequer. During these years he was still very poor and when in London took lodgings in Kentish Town whilst his wife stayed with a jeweller friend in Fleet Ditch.

John Reynolds, a poet and comic writer of the day, whose father was a prominent solicitor at Bromley in Kent and was often visited by Erskine, gave this description of him: "The young student resided in small lodgings near Hampstead, and openly avowed that he lived on cow-beef, because he could not afford any of a superior quality, dressed shabbily, expressed the greatest gratitude to Mr Harris for occasional free admission to Covent Garden, and used boastingly to exclaim to my father, 'Thank fortune, out of my own family I don't know a lord'".

Bentham, who had kept in touch with Erskine after reading his pamphlet on abuses in the army, confirmed his inability to dress well. "He was", he wrote, "so shabbily dressed as to be quite remarkable". He went on to add that his own determination not to practise law "astonished" Erskine who delighted in the prospect.[8] Bentham was, of course, wealthy and preferred to channel his genius into striving to reform the law - to Erskine a luxury which he neither desired nor could afford. However, Erskine's transition from rags to riches, worthy of *The Arabian Nights,* was not far away.

He took his honorary degree of MA at Cambridge in June 1778 and on July 3 of that year he was called to the Bar by Lincoln's Inn.

---

8.   *Works.* x. 565.

CHAPTER 3

Forensic Triumphs

The Seamen's Hospital Case

Despite achieving his goal Erskine might well have pondered on the dismal future which lay before a poor, newly-qualified barrister. However, that was not his way - he was ever full of self-confidence. And, almost at once, fate intervened to bring him his first case and give him a superb opening to make his name. Nonetheless, luck alone was not sufficient; he was eager to seize his chances. He had no useful connexion with solicitors, then called attorneys, and it seemed unlikely that any briefs would come his way for some time. But abuses came to his aid again. This time not in the army but in the famous Greenwich Hospital for Seamen.

Captain Baillie became the spark. This old salt was a respected veteran sailor who had been appointed Lieutenant-Governor of the charity. Here he uncovered serious corruption in breach of its Royal Charter. Accordingly, he presented petitions to the directors of the hospital, to the governors and, ultimately, to the Lords of the Admiralty asking for a full inquiry. Not one responded. Without regard to the risk to himself he then published an exposure of the corruption involved, including the denial of food to patients. This reflected, amongst others, on Lord Sandwich, who was First Lord of the Admiralty, and who, for electioneering purposes, had improperly placed in the hospital a great many of his cronies from his country estate. With perception and wit the poet Charles Churchill wrote of him that he,

"wrought sin with greediness and sought for shame with greater zeal than good men seek for fame".[1]

Lord Sandwich's career was indeed disreputable and had been since the 1760s when he was prominent in the orgies of the obscene "Hell-Fire Club" with the later more scrupulous John Wilkes. And although he shunned the spotlight of Baillie's exposures he made sure that the Board of Admiralty suspended the worthy captain. Some of his Lordship's placemen in the hospital, who had never even been to sea,[2] then secured from the Court of King's Bench a rule (ie, an interlocutory *ex parte* ruling) to show cause why a criminal information should not be filed against Baillie for libelling them.

At this point, purely by accident, Baillie and Erskine who were unknown to each other were both invited to a large dinner party. The Greenwich Hospital case was mentioned at table and Erskine, who was not aware that Captain Baillie was present, launched into an eloquent tirade against the corrupt and tyrannical practices of Lord Sandwich. On hearing this Captain Baillie inquired who

---

1.   *Rosciad.* 1763.
2.   The Hospital's Charter provided that, "all officers to be employed in the said Hospital be seafaring men, or such who have lost their limbs or been otherwise disabled in the sea service".

the young man was and, being informed that he was a recently called barrister and a former sailor, swore that he would have him as one of his counsel.

As it happened, they parted without being introduced to each other. The following day, whilst sitting in his chambers in a rare mood of depression at his prospects, Erskine was surprised to receive a retainer in the case of *Rex v. Baillie* together with a golden guinea. A coin which, incidentally, he always kept to show to his friends and acquaintances as his first fee.

Assuming he was to be the sole counsel for the defendant Erskine was disturbed on receiving his brief some time later to find that there were four other barristers instructed with him, all, of course, his senior. The opportunity of making a name for himself in court appeared to have evaporated. It was unlikely that he would be able to say more than a few formal words.

At a conference with the barristers in chambers which Baillie attended, three of the barristers urged a compromise which had been suggested by the plaintiffs. This was that the case should be withdrawn with the defendant paying all the costs of both sides to the dispute. "My advice, gentlemen", said Erskine, "may savour more of my late profession than my present, but I am against consenting". "I'll be damned if I do", said Baillie, and he hugged Erskine in his arms, exclaiming, "You are the man for me". How right he was to prove to be.

When the case came on for hearing in the King's Bench in Westminster Hall with Lord Mansfield presiding on November 23, 1778,[3] the defence barristers senior to Erskine all made long, dreary speeches by the end of which darkness had descended upon the courtroom.

---

3.   *State Trials.* xxi. 1. 1814.

Mansfield, tired and believing that all the defence counsel had spoken, indicated that the case would be adjourned until the following morning. Had he not done so Erskine would merely have made a short statement that evening and remained in obscurity. However, the adjournment provided him with a heaven-sent opportunity to sit up during the night and prepare a full speech of his own.

Odious Prosecution

On the re-assembling of the court the following day, with the Solicitor-General ready to proceed for the plaintiffs, a young barrister, unknown to almost all those present, rose and in a soft, but firm, voice said:

> My Lord; I am likewise of counsel for the author of this supposed libel, and if the matter for consideration had been merely a question of private wrong, in which the interests of society were no further concerned, than in the protection of the innocent, I should have thought myself well justified, after the very able defence made by the learned gentlemen who have spoken before me, in sparing your Lordship, already fatigued with the subject, and in leaving my client to the prosecution counsel and the judgment of the court.
>
> But upon an occasion of this serious and dangerous complexion, when a British subject is brought before a court of justice only for having ventured to attack abuses, which owe their continuance to the danger of attacking them ... I cannot relinquish the high privilege of defending [my client] - I will not give up even my small share of the honour of repelling and of exposing so odious a prosecution.

Unlike some others who were justly brought before the courts on charges of libel, Erskine continued, Captain Baillie had merely been doing his duty.

The defendant was not a disappointed malicious informer, prying into official abuses because without office himself, but himself a man in office; not troublesomely inquisitive into other men's departments, but conscientiously correcting his own at the risk of his office, from which the effrontery of power has already suspended him without proof of his guilt; a conduct not only unjust and illiberal, but highly disrespectful to this court, whose Judges sit in the double capacity of ministers of the law, and governors of this sacred and abused institution.[4] Indeed, Lord Sandwich has, in my mind, acted such a part -

At this point Lord Mansfield, observing that counsel was growing heated and personal about the First Lord of the Admiralty, reminded him that Lord Sandwich was not before the court. To which Erskine without hesitation replied that he knew he was not formally before the court, but for that very reason he would bring him before the court.

"He has placed these men", (the plaintiffs), he continued with eloquent invective, "in the front of the battle, in hopes to escape under their shelter, but I will not join in battle with them; *their* vices, though screwed up to the highest pitch of human depravity, are not of dignity enough to vindicate the combat with *me*. I will drag *him* to light, who is the dark mover behind this scene of iniquity".

---

4.   Many high officers of the law were indeed governors of the Hospital.

The Earl of Sandwich, he said, should disavow the acts of the prosecutors and restore Captain Baillie to his command. In doing so his offence would be no more than the all too common one of having allowed his own personal interest to prevail over his public duty in placing his voters in the hospital.

"But", he thundered, "if, on the contrary, he continues to protect the prosecutors, in spite of the evidence of their guilt,[5] which has excited the abhorrence of the numerous audience that crowd this court, if he keeps this injured man suspended, or dares to turn that suspension into a removal, I shall then not scruple to declare him an accomplice in their guilt, a shameless oppressor, a disgrace to his rank, and a traitor to his trust".

After this onslaught, Erskine then appealed to the Judges not to be content with doing their judicial duty in discharging the rule but to ensure that the defendant was restored to his position and not ruined for discharging his duty.

He now spoke to the Judges, he explained, not as an advocate alone but as a man. We would all be lost, he said, if the Fleet were to be crippled by abuses. "If the seaman, who, while he exposes his body to fatigues and dangers, looking forward to Greenwich as an asylum for infirmity and old age, sees the gates of it blocked up by corruption, and hears the riot and mirth of luxurious landsmen, who by the express words of the Hospital's Charter are not permitted to be there, drowning the groans and complaints of the wounded, helpless companions of his glory, he will tempt the seas no more".

---

5.   For instance, Mr Ibbetson, confidential clerk of the Admiralty, had reduced the pensioners' wards in order to provide accommodation for himself and his footmen.

After stating that the Admiralty could take over the bodies but not the minds of seamen he proceeded to say of Baillie, "Fine and imprisonment! The man deserves a palace, instead of a prison, who prevents the palace, built by the public bounty of his country, from being converted into a dungeon, and who sacrifices his own security in the interests of humanity and virtue".

When the Captain was turned out of office, Erskine continued, pensioner Charles Smith had testified, in an affidavit which Erskine thanked God he could not read without tears, that he had been expelled from the infirmary when sick. As a direct consequence his unfortunate wife and his helpless innocent children died in want and misery, the poor woman actually expiring at the gates of the hospital.

Erskine then resigned his client, he said, into the hands of the Judges with well-founded confidence and hope. This was because the torrent of corruption overwhelming other parts of the Constitution would be checked in the courtroom by the sacred independence of the Judges. He knew the court would determine according to the law. Yet, if the sentence was adverse to his client he would nevertheless bow to it.

But then he would not scruple to say that it was high time for every honest man to remove himself from a country in which he could no longer do his duty to the public with safety. Where cruelty and inhumanity were suffered to dishonour virtue, and where vice passed through a court of justice unpunished and unrebuked.

Perhaps not surprisingly, after the power of this youthful eloquence, the rule was discharged with costs for Captain Baillie.

"Trance of Amazement"

On reading Erskine's speech it is difficult to remember that this was his first case.[6] It proved to be an inspiring and auspicious start to his career. Of course, we have to remember that counsel were then more flamboyant in their use of language and in their approach than is normally the case today. But Erskine was a tyro in public speaking on this occasion and he spoke after four senior counsel who might be thought to have said all that could be said for their client.

He was called to order by the Lord Chief Justice but persisted - improperly - in his crushing denunciation of Lord Sandwich, which appears to have been supported by the public in the court. His peroration was masterly, combining submission with defiance and spoken with a quietness that secured the attention of everyone present. *The Edinburgh Review*, in a later notice of some of Erskine's speeches, observed that by this speech Erskine, at the very outset of his brilliant career, had astonished the legal world with a display of talents, which was outshone, but not obscured, by his later, riper efforts.

It also said that his vigorous attack on prosecution witnesses showed that his professional courage was not acquired after his later success which made it a "safe and cheap virtue" but was displayed at a moment when he was taking the most formidable risks.[7]

Joseph Jekyll, a barrister and Member of Parliament, coming by chance into the court, said he found the whole

---

6.   As with all Erskine's speeches only a small part can be quoted here, when often only reading the whole speech can reveal its breathtaking quality.
7.   Volume 16. 103. 1810.

court, Judges and all, "in a trance of amazement".[8]
Spectators pressed around Erskine to offer their
congratulations and, on walking through the Hall, he
received an ovation from attorneys, many of whom offered
him briefs on the spot.

Asked how he had the courage to stand up so manfully
to Lord Mansfield, he replied somewhat melodramatically
that he thought his little children were plucking his robe
and saying, "Now, father, is the time to get us bread".
Many years later he was to reveal that he had indeed
scarcely a shilling to his name when he received this first
retainer. However, from then on his future was secure.

It is a tribute to Erskine's skills and the fairness of
Lord Mansfield to observe that in an inquiry the following
year before the House of Lords into the same abuses at
the Hospital, their Lordships, against all the evidence,
decided by a majority that Captain Baillie's complaints
against the Earl of Sandwich were baseless.[9] He was, of
course, one of them.

Westminster Hall

We have noticed that the Court of the Lord Chief Justice
was held in the old Westminster Hall as were the Courts
of Common Pleas and Chancery. In the eighteenth
century this presented a bizarre spectacle. The Hall had
shops selling books, prints, gloves, etc., as well as stalls
with "nimble-tongued, painted seamstresses" selling
knick-knacks, on each side of its whole length, whilst the
Judges sat in open court. Rents and profits were paid to

---

8.   *Dictionary of National Biography.*
9.   *State Trials. Op. cit.*

the Warden of the Fleet prison.

The courts were, however, partitioned off from the body of the Hall to a height of eight feet, with side bars on the outside, at which the attorneys made their applications.

The Judges, jurors, witnesses and counsel were all constantly interrupted by the buzz of conversation and the general noise of shoppers and bystanders. Calls for silence to "women and lawyers" made by ushers proved ineffective. The whole solemnity of the courts must to some extent have been destroyed, amongst other diversions, by what a letter in *The Gentleman's Magazine* described as, "the flirtations with the seamstresses and the shopwomen".[10]

We may also note at this point that by statute the Master of the Rolls and the Lord Chief Baron each received a salary of £4,000 a year. That for puisne Judges and barons was £3,000 a year. These sums were considered to help retain the independence of the judiciary as the Judges no longer needed to seek money from outside sources as in the past.

On retirement Judges received annuities of between £2,000 and £3,000 per annum if they had served for 15 years, but a retiring Lord Chancellor received £4,000 a year for life regardless of the length of his term of office since he had no security of tenure and retired with an outgoing government. We shall see something later of what successful barristers were able to earn in the way of fees.

Admiral Keppel

After the Baillie triumph, briefs tumbled into Erskine's

---

10.   480. November 1853.

chambers in an ever increasing flow. He continued to practise in the King's Bench where he often appeared before Lord Mansfield whom he always treated with respect but with an independence necessary to advance the cases of his clients.

But there were other venues, and in January 1779 we find him appearing for Admiral Lord Keppel in his celebrated courts-martial at Portsmouth. The prosecution was meant to secure Keppel's ignominious execution as a scapegoat in the manner of the innocent Admiral Byng some years earlier. It will be recalled that Voltaire immortalized Byng with his bitter witticism in *Candide* that in England it "pays to shoot an admiral from time to time to encourage the others".[11] However, in Keppel's case the prosecution had reckoned without Erskine.

Keppel was commander of the Home Fleet aboard HMS *Victory* and had proved to be a formidable combatant in his blockade of Brest in Brittany. The indictment against him was in reality brought by Sir Hugh Palliser on behalf of Lord Sandwich who was an unbending foe of Keppel in Parliament and used the power of the Admiralty to pursue him as well as Baillie. It charged that Keppel was guilty of incapacity and misconduct in the battle with the French fleet off Ushant. The trial lasted 13 days and Erskine, the former sailor, was in his element. He never wearied for a moment in his efforts to assist the Admiral.

Most commanders of ships who had been active in the engagement gave evidence favourable to their Admiral. But the testimony of Captain Alexander Hood of HMS *Robust,* who was second in command to Palliser's line, was hostile. However, in the course of questioning he was obliged to admit that he had made alterations to his log-

---

11.   Chapter xxiii. 1759.

book. The log of HMS *Formidable* was then found to have
had three of its pages torn out and a false page inserted.
Lord Sandwich was widely believed to be involved in
these serious breaches of naval discipline.

By the law of the time counsel was not permitted to
examine the witnesses or address the courts-martial. But
Erskine framed questions to be put by his client and
prepared the speech which Keppel was allowed to deliver
to the court himself. According to *The Gentleman's
Magazine,* Erskine "personally examined all the Admirals
and Captains of the fleet, and satisfied himself that he
could substantiate the innocence of his client, before the
speech which he had written for him was read".[12]

On his way to the trial Keppel's prestige in the navy
was illustrated by the enthusiastic cheering of sailors
lining the streets of Portsmouth. And in his address to
the courts-martial he pointed out that when he had
returned to England after the battle of Ushant no less
than the King himself had received him with great
respect. Even the First Lord of the Admiralty had praised
his conduct of the battle.

As for Sir Hugh Palliser, he had not hesitated to sail
with Keppel on another voyage and, at home, had written
letters to him approving his actions at Ushant. Then,
after a considerable lapse of time, the same Palliser who
himself disobeyed orders during the battle, had produced
five articles charging negligence against his Admiral. A
most ingenious mode of proceeding, observed Keppel.

Indeed, "An accusation against a commander-in-chief",
he declared, "might draw off public attention from neglect
of duty in an inferior officer. I could almost wish, in pity
to my accuser, that appearances were not so strong

---

12.   Memoire of Erskine.

against him". Continuing the offensive against his prosecutor, the Admiral continued:

> The trial has left my accuser without excuse, and he now cuts that sort of figure which I trust in God all accusers of innocence will ever exhibit! As to this court, I entreat you, gentlemen, who compose it, to recollect that you sit here as a court of honour, as well as a court of justice; and I now stand before you, not merely to save my life, but for a purpose of infinitely greater moment - to clear my name. My conscience is perfectly clear - I have no secret machination, no dark contrivance, to answer for. My heart does not reproach me. As to my enemies, I would not wish the greatest enemy I have in the world to be afflicted with so heavy a punishment as my accuser's conscience.

Public Acclaim

When Keppel concluded his speech, the courtroom resounded with shouts of approval. Unanimously, the court honourably acquitted him of the charge, affirming that, far from having sullied the honour of the navy, he had acted as a brave, judicious and experienced officer.[13] Overnight Keppel became a public hero.

Portsmouth turned out in his honour. Then, on two successive nights the streets of the cities of London and Westminster were alight with bonfires in an atmosphere bordering on riot. Sir Hugh Palliser suffered from having

---

13.   Lord Nelson was less than enthusiastic, however, saying "I will not lead my fleet as Keppel did". *Nelson Despatches.* v. On the other hand he may have been referring to changes in techniques of warfare at sea by his time.

his house broken into by the crowds who destroyed his furniture and burnt him in effigy. In alarm he wrote to Lord Sandwich that his life was in danger. The Whigs in Parliament, many of whom had been noisily partisan in the courtroom, hailed the verdict that the charges had been "malicious and ill-founded" as a blow to the government.

The House of Commons joined the fray and voted the nation's thanks to Keppel for his distinguished courage, conduct and ability in defending the Kingdom. And, taking full advantage of the situation, Josiah Wedgwood produced thousands of cameos and busts of the Admiral, whilst Sir Joshua Reynolds painted four portraits of him, one of them for Erskine and another for Edmund Burke.

Patriotic inn-keepers in many parts of the country had signs made bearing pictures of Keppel's head. And his name is still honoured on The Hard at Portsmouth, where an hotel is named after him which exhibits some of his original papers. Beyond the hotel can now be seen the tall masts and rigging of HMS *Victory* which also became Nelson's flagship. At the time this inn was a favourite with sailors who called it "The Nut",[14] to distinguish it from other "Keppel's Heads" across the land. And with poetic justice, Keppel himself afterwards became First Lord of the Admiralty with a seat in the Cabinet.

As for Erskine, there was little publicity for him from the case since he could not represent the defendant, but he received a magnificent present of £1,000 from his elated client. "Do me the favour", the Admiral wrote to his counsel, "to accept the enclosed notes" (two bank notes of £500 each) "as an acknowledgment of the zealous and indefatigable industry you have shown in the long and

---

14.   Sailors' nickname for Keppel owing to his eccentricity.

tedious course of my courts-martial. I shall be happy, if I have been in any degree the means of furnishing you with opportunities of showing those talents, which only wanted to be made known to carry you to the summit of your profession".

A delighted Erskine called upon the Admiral in person to offer his thanks, but finding him not at home wrote a generous reply attesting to the honour he felt in having assisted him. The honour was, he wrote, one which he would always consider as "the brightest and happiest in my life". In good humour he then hurried to Bromley to show his reward to his acquaintances there and exclaimed, "*Voila!* the nonsuit of *cow* beef, my good friends".[15]

Bar of the House of Commons

Before long Erskine had the new experience of being retained as counsel at the bar of the House of Commons to argue the case against a Bill which would have a dampening effect upon the freedom of the press. By letters patent from James I, the Stationers' Company and the Universities of Oxford and Cambridge had long enjoyed a monopoly in printing almanacs. This was ignored, in 1779, by Thomas Carnan, a bookseller in St Paul's Churchyard, who published his own almanacs which were cheaper, more complete and more accurate.

In legal proceedings for an injunction against Carnan, the Court of Common Pleas and the Court of Exchequer both ruled that the royal grant was void. They refused to accept the validity of the letters patent on the ground that

---

15.   Campbell. *Op.cit.* 403.

almanacs were not public ordinances. Lord North, who was Prime Minister and as it happens also Chancellor of the University of Oxford, thereupon introduced a Bill into Parliament to revest the monopoly in the original parties. Carnan was generally considered to have a forlorn hope of the Bill being rejected. But he chose Erskine as his counsel.

Erskine's speech to the House of Commons against the Bill was so cogent that the House remained crowded throughout its length. He argued that every unnecessary restraint on the natural liberty of mankind was a tyranny which no wise legislature would inflict. The Glorious Revolution had heralded the great era of the liberty of the press, freed from the prerogative of the Crown and courts such as the Star Chamber whose literary constables had been the Company of Stationers itself. This prerogative court had suppressed all the science and information which could lead to freedom. With the legislature he was addressing, he said, he felt no likelihood of the press being restrained by monopolies, but "who can look into the future?" The Bill was a consistent piece of tyranny, absurdity and falsehood.

That the Bill was rejected by a majority of 45 votes upon a division immediately after he had left the bar was ascribed solely to Erskine's eloquence. Lord Eliot, who was MP for Cornwall, had travelled to London to support the Bill at the request of his brother-in-law, Lord North. In the event he voted against, declaring in the lobby that, "after Mr Erskine's speech I found it impossible to do otherwise".

However, Lord John Campbell, in his *Lives of the Chancellors*, suspected that the result was achieved by a government promise to indemnify the monopoly-holders for their loss out of the public revenue.[16] This could not be so, however, since the suggestion of compensating the Universities was made by Erskine himself at the conclusion of his speech and the hint was taken up by the government only after the vote. Bearing in mind that most Members were "sons" of the two Universities, Erskine had suggested that the advantage they would lose should be, "repaired to them by the bounty of the Crown, or by your own. It were much better that the people of England should pay £10,000 a year to each of them, than suffer them to enjoy one farthing at the expense of the ruin of a free citizen, or the monopoly of a free trade".

Duelling

Erskine's next appearance before the King's Bench was as counsel for a naval lieutenant, Bourne, who had challenged to a duel his commanding officer, Admiral Sir James Wallace. At common law, unless a duel was fought in hot blood on a sudden falling out, a man who killed his opponent was held to be guilty of murder.[17] Yet, although it offended the sensibilities of many people, duelling was still quite common in the eighteenth century. Apparently, Bourne had been badly treated by his commander (although his own conduct was provocative) and considered himself honour bound to make the challenge. When it was declined he struck the Admiral with his cane and inflicted a severe wound on his head.

Erskine used all his skills to defend his client and even

---

16.   *Op.cit.* 404.
17.   Coke. 3rd Institute. 157/8. 1644.

went so far as to identify himself with his defiance. Indeed, he declared that the defendant's conduct was so full of merit that he himself, in similar circumstances, would have pursued his old commander, Sir John Lindsay, with the same vigour.

Although he had once fought a duel in which fortunately neither party was hurt, Erskine accepted in court that private duelling was an offence against the laws of God and destructive of good government. It was a practice by which the most amiable man in society might be lost by an inglorious death, depending upon mere chance.

"But", he added, "though I feel all this as I think a Christian and a humane man ought to feel it, yet I am not ashamed to acknowledge that I would rather be pilloried by the court in every square in London, than obey the law of England, which I thus profess so highly to respect, in a case, where that custom, which I have reprobated, warned me that the public voice was in the other scale".

He believed, he said, that every man who heard him would feel the same, for without the respect and good opinion of the world we live in, life itself was a worse imprisonment than any which the laws could inflict. "And the closest dungeon to which a court of justice can send an offender, is far better with the secret pity and even approbation of those that send him there, than the rage of the universe with the contempt and scorn of its inhabitants".

He then pleaded the infirmities of human nature, with a young military man before the court jealous of his fame and honour who had been treated with the grossest indignity by his superior officer. He admitted a crime had been committed in the eyes of the law, yet hoped, he said, for a mild sentence based upon what would be secretly felt by the court, rather than what he might decently express from the Bar.

Counsel for Admiral Wallace asked the court, "to forget, for a little while, the laws of chivalry and the wild maxims of romance" with which it had been so liberally entertained by Erskine. This sparked off Mr Justice Willes who claimed that Erskine had lost himself in the wilds of chivalry and adopted the romantic notions of a knight-errant. In the event, for the assault, Lieutenant Bourne was imprisoned for two years and had to find sureties for good behaviour for seven years.

CHAPTER 4

High Treason and Sedition

The Gordon Riots

Although still only in his second year at the Bar, Erskine had now arrived at an important turning point in his career with the defence of Lord George Gordon on a charge of high treason. To understand the full triumph of his speech, however, it is necessary to look first at the Gordon Riots themselves.

Lord George Gordon was an ignorant young nobleman, almost simple-minded in his attitude to Catholics. Unfortunately, he was elected President of the Protestant Association in which capacity he attended the House of Commons on Friday, June 2, 1780, with a petition praying for the repeal of the recently enacted Catholic Relief Act. Few anticipated the huge crowd of 40,000 people that would accompany him, or its vicious nature.

The crowd blockaded the entrances to both Houses of Parliament and no Member was allowed to enter until he had shouted, "No popery! No popery!". Several Lords, MPs and Bishops who declined to do so were kicked and knocked down. The Bishop of Lincoln escaped only by hiding in a nearby house, changing his clothes and climbing over the roofs of adjoining dwellings. Lord Sandwich had his coach windows broken, his face cut open, and was forced to turn back. Lords Townsend and Hillsborough both had their wigs torn off and their bags stolen. Lord Stormont suffered the misfortune of having his coach smashed to pieces.

Provocatively, Lord George Gordon encouraged the crowds with anti-Catholic harangues and denounced to them some Members as they arrived, including Edmund Burke. Other Members tried to persuade him to keep quiet but he only appealed the more to his supporters. Eventually, soldiers dispersed the demonstrators from the precincts of Parliament but they simply turned to pillaging a number of Catholic chapels.

London Burning

Saturday was fairly quiet, but on Sunday the violent rioting broke out again and this time the terrified Lord Mayor took no action, except to confine the troops to barracks. This step met with the approval of a craven government paralysed with fear. As a consequence the district of Moorfields, where many Catholics lived, saw chapels and private houses looted and set on fire until the locality was gutted. The following day Smithfield and Wapping suffered the same fate and the City was swiftly swept with destruction.

Readers of Charles Dickens's novel, *Barnaby Rudge*, will recall its vivid description of the riots in which Newgate prison was stormed and destroyed, and the houses of Mr Justice Cox, Sir John Fielding and Lord Mansfield burnt down. Much of London was now afire whilst the authorities continued to stand by, petrified and idle.

The King's Bench and Fleet prisons suffered the same fate as Newgate, and more houses, shops and factories of Catholics were looted and fired. At Langdale's distillery in Holborn the vats were forced open and raw spirits flowed in streams down the gutters of the street. Drunken men and women were lying about the roadway in a stupor when the alcohol caught fire from a blazing house and caused carnage.

"In the darkness of the night", recalled the *Annual Register,*

> was one of the most dreadful spectacles this country has ever beheld ... at the same instant flames ascending and rolling in clouds from the King's Bench and Fleet Prisons, from New Bridewell, from the tollgate on Blackfriars Bridge, from houses in every quarter of the town, and particularly from the bottom and middle of Holborn, where the conflagration was horrible beyond description ... Six-and-thirty fires all blazing at one time, and in different quarters of the city, were to be seen from one spot.[1]

Whilst Samuel Romilly stood sentry throughout these dark nights at Gray's Inn, Erskine turned back some marauding rioters at the Temple with a suitable display of arms and determination. Indeed, he offered to defend Lord Mansfield's house if given command of a body of troops but his suggestion was rejected.

The real turning point came only when the rioters received their first serious check in failing to capture the Bank of England which was defended by a small force

1.   261. 1788.

collected by the City Chamberlain, John Wilkes. Under pressure from Wilkes the Lord Mayor now belatedly deployed troops and the convulsion was to be all over by the 14th. The calamity encouraged by the former inertia was plain for all to see. Many hundreds were left dead. London lay desolated and the foundations of government shaken.

Despite all this, some people thought Lord George Gordon was to be pitied particularly as during the riots he had made an attempt to restore order, although by then things had gone too far. But the great majority of citizens from whom juries were drawn had feared for their lives, their families and their properties. Things looked bleak for his Lordship then when he was arrested, committed to the Tower and indicted for high treason in levying war against the Crown. All the power and majesty of the law were to be used against him. But Erskine was one of the counsel for the prisoner.

The Trial

Lord George Gordon was brought to trial in the King's Bench before Lord Mansfield and other Judges on February 5, 1781.[2] Ominously, 21 rioters had already been tried and hanged.

Clearly a task of immense difficulty faced Erskine as the case for the Crown was opened by the Attorney-General who led the elite of the Bar. But in cross-examining the Crown witnesses who gave evidence he managed to reduce the convoluted evidence of some of them to ridicule. However, against the prosecution case

---

2.   *State Trials. Op.cit.* 485.

Lloyd Kenyon, afterwards Lord Chief Justice, then made a poor speech for the defence. He was, in fact, a curious choice for the role of leading for the defence since he was an equity lawyer with little experience of public speaking or constitutional issues.

Sensing that his leader had confused the jury, Erskine requested leave to postpone his speech until after the evidence of witnesses for the prisoner had been given instead of adopting the usual practice of following immediately after Kenyon. As a precedent he quoted only a single case from the *State Trials* but his request was granted and 12 witnesses testified to the excellent character of the accused, his loyalty to the King and attachment to the Constitution. On the other hand, what they had to say about the riots when they were cross-examined did nothing to assist the defence case.

Erskine rose a little after midnight and quickly dispelled any feeling of exhaustion in the minds of the Judges and jury with a captivating speech. This was the first time he had addressed a jury. He commenced by telling them that he was a young man with little experience, not used to the bar of criminal courts, and sinking under a dreadful consciousness of his defects. But, in weaving his spell he added, "I have, however, this consolation, that no ignorance nor inattention on my part can possibly prevent you from seeing ... that the Crown has established no case of treason".

Constructive Treason

He proceeded to outline the law of treason, as set out in the still operative Statute of Treason passed in the reign of Edward III and the oppressive extensions of it that flowed from constructions of its provisions by the courts over the succeeding centuries. In fact, the Act had provided that no amendments of it should be made except by Parliament - but this had been ignored by the Judges.

Then, referring to the destruction of Lord Mansfield's house in the riots, Erskine asked if anyone could possibly believe that Lord George Gordon could have incited the mob to burn down the house of that "great and venerable magistrate, who has presided so long in that high tribunal, that the oldest of us do not remember him with any other impression than as an awful form and figure of justice". He was, he pointedly reminded the jury, a Judge who had always been a friend of Protestant dissenters. It was not credible that a man of noble birth and liberal education such as the accused could possibly have consented to such a deed.

Erskine accepted that the prisoner had assembled the multitude to accompany him to the Houses of Parliament of which he was a Member. But he denied that he had assembled them in hostile array or with any intention of using force, which had to be proved for a charge of treason to be successful.

Neither side called as a witness the self-taught Suffolk poet, George Crabbe who, going about the town on his own business, saw near the Old Bailey some 500 men accompanying Lord George Gordon, "bowing as he passed along in a coach drawn by the mob".[3]

Erskine reviewed all the evidence given, varying his tone from mild explanation to furious invective. Then, after mentioning the prisoner's offer to the government to quell the disturbance, he exclaimed, "I say, by God, that man is a ruffian, who shall, after this, presume to build upon such honest, artless conduct, as an evidence

---

3.   *The Faber Book of Reportage.* ed. John Carey. 238. 1987.

of guilt".

This apparently unprecedented use of the name of the Almighty in a court of law in a voice filled with emotion was a daring appeal to the feelings of the jury and it produced what *The Edinburgh Review* described as a "sensation quite electrical which baffled all power of description". It was thought to have been unpremeditated. Indeed, the *Review* went on to make the somewhat exaggerated claim that an, "intuitive and momentary impulse alone could have prompted a flight, which it alone could sustain; and as its failure would indeed have been fatal, so its eminent success must be allowed to rank it among the most famous feats of oratory".[4]

The use of the word "ruffian" to describe the prosecution counsel and witnesses also caused consternation. It was, said the Solicitor-General, a licentious and unprecedented slur upon the prosecutors and their witnesses. He complained that even if a learned gentleman at the Bar told him 16 times a day to his face that he was a ruffian, he did not deserve it and would not allow such abuse to frighten him from doing his duty as an English advocate. However, Erskine refused to retract, qualify or explain away his remark.

After attacking the evidence for the Crown and dwelling on the testimony in support of the innocence of the prisoner who he claimed had not himself resorted to force and violence, Erskine then appealed to the jury:

What, then, has produced this trial for high treason? What! but the inversion of all justice, by judging from consequences, instead of from causes and designs? What! but the artful manner in which the Crown has endeavoured to blend the petitioners in a body, and the

---

4.   xvi. 108. April 1810.

zeal with which an animated disposition conducted it, with the melancholy crimes that followed - crimes which the shameful indolence of our magistrates, which the total extinction of all police and all government suffered to be committed in broad day, in the delirium of drunkenness, by an unarmed banditti, without a head, without plan or object, and without a refuge from the instant grip of justice; a banditti, with whom the associated Protestants and their President had no manner of connexion, and whose cause they overturned, dishonoured, and ruined? ...

Do they wish, while you are listening to the evidence, to connect it with consequences in spite of reason and truth, to hang the millstone of prejudice round his innocent neck to sink him? If there be such men, may God forgive them for the attempt, and inspire you with fortitude and wisdom to do your duty to your fellow-citizens with calm, steady, reflecting minds.

I may now, therefore, relieve you from the pain of hearing me any longer, and be myself relieved from a subject which agitates and distresses me ... I shall make no address to your passions. I will not remind you of the long and rigorous imprisonment he has suffered; I will not speak to you of his great youth, of his illustrious birth, or of his uniformly animated and generous zeal in Parliament for the Constitution of his country. Such topics might be useful in the balance of a doubtful case. At present, the plain and rigid rules of justice and truth are sufficient to entitle me to your verdict.

You will then restore my innocent client to liberty, and me to that peace of mind, which, since the protection of his innocence in any part depended on me, I have never known.

We have the words. The clarity of his arguments, the force of his reasoning, the eloquence of language and the application of the evidence to the principles he was advocating. It is a pity we cannot know the thrilling sensations they produced on the jury. These emotions and the subtle suggestion that the jury had already decided the verdict meant in the event that they paid little heed to the reply of the Solicitor-General or the severe summing up of Lord Mansfield at 5.15 a.m. As it turned out their unanimous verdict was - Not Guilty.

All the world seem pleased. Dr Johnson captured the significance of the verdict when he said that he was glad Lord George Gordon had escaped, rather than that a precedent should be set for hanging a man for *constructive treason*. Which, Boswell added, "in consistency with his true, manly, Constitutional Toryism, he considered would be a dangerous engine of arbitrary power".[5]

Constructive treason is what the charge really amounted to and such artificial treasons were widely regarded as highly threatening and injurious to public freedom. As Erskine had pointedly made clear, constructive extensions of the penal law of the Statute of Treason by the Judges had made the criminality of an act depend upon its *consequences* rather than upon its *nature*.

It is noteworthy that as a result of this case jurors became more and more unwilling to convict for constructive treasons. However, the response of an obdurate government was simply to bring in a statute to incorporate such judge-made constructions into the enacted law.[6]

---

5.   *Life of Johnson. Op.cit.* 1132.
6.   36 Geo.III. c.7.

The Case of the Dean of St Asaph

By the year 1783 Erskine had still been a mere five years at the Bar. Yet such had become his eminence in the King's Bench in this time that Lord Mansfield suggested he be given a patent of precedence to become a silk. This distinction was conferred upon him in May of that year. Prior to that, "juniors" who were older than he were unable to be retained with him and his promotion was received therefore with relief by some and pleasure by all.

Now began his special retainers which took him to assizes in all parts of the country with a fee of at least 300 guineas for each case. Apparently the high fees were meant to prevent an unseemly scramble for business, although it is difficult to see how. In the event, the first of his special retainers was in the case of the Dean of St Asaph.

In the year 1783, soon after (for Britain) the ignominious end of the American War of Independence, public opinion in England turned to the urgent necessity of reforming the evils in the system of representation of the people in the House of Commons. Rotten boroughs were an open disgrace as was the lack of franchise for many large towns. In consequence, William Pitt, the Prime Minister, brought the subject before Parliament although a few years later, under the impact of the French Revolution, he was to the fore in upholding the old system and persecuting those who had failed to turn with him.

In support of such reform Sir William Jones, a well-known barrister in London and afterwards a Judge at the Supreme Court at Bengal, published a small tract entitled "A Dialogue between a Farmer and a Country Gentleman on the Principles of Government". This dealt with the virtues of government and defects in the representation of the people. Sir William's father-in-law, Dr William Shipley, the Dean of St Asaph, recommended the Dialogue to a society of reformers in Wales, and, having seen it attacked by the court party, had it reprinted in the Welsh language with his own preface suggesting that it was just, rational and constitutional.

In an angry response, the Honourable Mr Fitzmaurice, brother to the first Marquis of Lansdowne, preferred a bill of indictment against the Dean for seditious libel. The seditious purpose was alleged to be to excite disloyalty and disaffection against the King and an armed rebellion against the State. Yet, so little merit did the allegations have that both the Attorney-General and the Solicitor-General had previously declined to prosecute on behalf of the government.

Advocate and Citizen

The case was to be heard at Wrexham in the summer of 1783 before Lord Kenyon, by now Chief Justice of Chester. Erskine had travelled 200 miles to appear for the defence when it was discovered that a paper had been circulated in the neighbourhood which argued that in all cases of libel the jury were judges of law as well as of fact.

The prosecution argued that this would prejudice the trial and asked for a postponement. The Dean swore an affidavit denying all knowledge of the paper. Erskine made the point that the prosecution's motion was unreasonable and that delay would cause his client extreme hardship. He said also that a letter written by the prosecutor could be produced which would show he was acting vindictively. Ignoring these claims, and acting with indecent haste, the Chief Justice postponed the case. In the spring of 1784 the hearing was then removed by the prosecutor's writ of *certiorari* into the Court of King's Bench. However, it was ultimately tried at Shrewsbury that summer before Mr Justice Buller.

Edward Bearcroft, leading counsel for the prosecution, first described the dialogue as a libel. Having done so he then argued that this was not a question for the jury since they were bound to convict the defendant simply if they believed he caused it to be published - which was not denied. The object of the pamphlet, he said, was to persuade the public that every man of age had a right to choose his own representative in Parliament. With a self-assurance to be wondered at he then continued, "I have no difficulty to say that the man who maintains this proposition is either a fool or a knave. If he believes it himself he is an idiot; if he does not he is a dishonest man".

In his reply Erskine insisted on the right of the jury to decide whether the publication was or was not a libel. He pointed out to them that the prosecution had ventured to charge the Dean with the seditious purpose of exciting disloyalty to the King and an armed rebellion against the State. Yet all the prosecution evidence amounted to was nothing more than publishing the Dialogue which contained nothing seditious and had the Dean's preface which contained a solemn protest against all sedition.

The only difficulty which I feel, claimed Erskine, in resisting so false and malevolent an accusation, is to be able to repress the feeling excited by its folly and injustice, within those bounds which may leave my faculties their natural and unclouded operations; for I solemnly declare to you, that if he had been indicted as a libeller of our holy religion, only for publishing that the world was made by its Almighty author, my astonishment could not have been greater than it is at this moment, to see that little book which I hold in my hand, presented by a Grand Jury of English subjects as a libel upon the government of England. Every sentiment contained in it ... is to be found in the brightest pages of English literature, and in the most sacred volume of English laws: if any one sentence, from the beginning to the end of it, be seditious or libellous, the Bill of Rights was a seditious libel; the Revolution was a wicked rebellion; the existing government is a traitorous conspiracy ...

At this point, Erskine re-asserted that his client had not committed a libel and said that he desired to be considered the fellow-criminal of the defendant, if by their verdict the jury found him to be one, since he intended to publish the sentiments contained in the book upon every suitable occasion. Identifying himself with his client in this way was something that endeared juries to this counsel.

Normally, he said, he kept the advocate and the private man apart. "But where the conviction of the private individual is the subversion or surrender of public privileges, the advocate has a more extensive charge - the duty of the patriot citizen then mixes itself with his obligation to his client, and he disgraces himself, dishonours his profession, and betrays his country if he does not vindicate the rights of all his fellow-citizens".

Erskine knew that Buller would take the correct legal position that it was for the Judge to decide whether or not a book was libellous and that the jury should decide only if it had been published. In order, therefore, to forestall judicial reproof at what he was proposing to argue to the contrary, he mischievously said to the jury: "When I reflect upon the danger which has often attended the liberty of the press in former times, from the arbitrary proceedings of abject, unprincipled, and dependent Judges ... I cannot help congratulate the public that you are to try this indictment with the assistance of the learned Judge before you, much too instructed in the laws of this land to mislead you by mistake, and too conscientious to misinstruct you by design".

The jury, he added, should preserve their independence by judging the *intention* which was the essence of every crime. Having been a pupil to the Judge before he was raised to the Bench, Erskine said, he anticipated nothing from him unfavourable to innocence.

Although the Dialogue contained only nine pages, and was in reality a small pamphlet, Erskine spent the next several hours examining it sentence by sentence to show that most Englishmen would agree with it.[7] In fact, he said, it was the foundation of the Prime Minister's Bill to reform representation in Parliament. Furthermore, after Sir William Jones had written the book he was appointed by the King to be a Judge of the Supreme Court at Bengal.

Erskine then explained the general law of libel to the jury and returned to the question of who was to decide whether a book was libellous or not. If, he said, you find the defendant guilty, not believing the book to be a libel, or the intention of the publisher seditious, your verdict and your opinion will be in conflict.

Prosecuting counsel, he continued, had drawn a line around them in saying, "Thus far shall you go" - he hoped with as much success as King Canute with the sea. But, he added, since Mr Bearcroft had thought proper to coop them in, it was his duty to let them out. If the Judge told them that the pamphlet was in the abstract a libel he

---

7.   No mention of Welshmen was made!

would not agree that they had to find the defendant guilty unless they also thought so. "Criminal justice in the hands of the people", he said, "is the basis of freedom. While that remains there can be no tyranny, because the people will not execute tyrannical laws against themselves".

Defiance by the Jury

As expected, Mr Justice Buller told the jury in his summing up that, there being no doubt as to the libel, the only question they had to decide was whether the defendant had or had not published the pamphlet. He expressed himself astonished at Erskine's contrary contention on a question of law so thoroughly established.

The jury retired for half an hour and, on their return, found the Dean guilty of publishing only. The following remarkable scene then took place:

Buller, J:	If you find him guilty of publishing, you must not say the word "only".
Erskine:	By that they mean to find there was no sedition.
Juror:	We only find him guilty of publishing. We do not find anything else.
Erskine:	I beg your Lordship's pardon; with great submission, I am sure I mean nothing that is irregular. I understand they say "We only find him guilty of publishing".
Juror:	Certainly, that is all we do find.
Buller, J:	If you only attend to what is said, there is no question or doubt.
Erskine:	Gentlemen, I desire to know whether you mean the word "only" to stand in your verdict.

Jurymen:	Certainly.
Buller, J:	Gentlemen, if you add the word "only" it will be negativing the libel.
Erskine:	I desire your Lordship sitting here as Judge to record the verdict as given by the jury. If the jury depart from the word "only", they alter their verdict.
Buller, J:	I will take the verdict as they mean to give it; it shall not be altered. Gentlemen, if I understand you right, your verdict is this, you mean to say guilty of publishing this libel?
Juror:	No; the pamphlet; we do not decide upon its being a libel.
Buller, J:	You say he is guilty of publishing the pamphlet, and that the meaning of the innuendoes is as stated in the indictment?
Juror:	Certainly.
Erskine:	Is the word "only" to stand part of the verdict?
Juror:	Certainly.
Erskine:	Then I insist it shall be recorded.
Buller, J:	Then the verdict must be misunderstood; let me understand the jury.
Erskine:	The jury do understand their verdict.
Buller, J:	Sir, I will not be interrupted.
Erskine:	I stand here as an advocate for a brother citizen, and I desire that the word *only* may be recorded.
Buller, J:	*Sit down, Sir; remember your duty, or I shall be obliged to proceed in another manner.*
Erskine:	*Your Lordship may proceed in what manner you think fit; I know my duty as*

well as your Lordship knows yours. I
shall not alter my conduct.

In consequence of this bullying by counsel the Judge
now seemed nonplussed what to do and the jury, confused
by what had taken place, withdrew and eventually
returned to enter a verdict, "Guilty of publishing, but
whether a libel or not we do not find". The Judge then
declared the Dean to be guilty on all counts.

Notwithstanding the decision Erskine had, in this one
case, defended the freedom of the press, asserted the right
of the jury to determine libel as a question of fact and
upheld the independence of the Bar. His speech to the
jury, declared Charles James Fox, was the finest piece of
reasoning in the English language. At least it was a fine
example of Erskine's ability to flatter a jury on their
intelligence and common sense since it was clearly
contrary to the law, as he well knew.

Legal Argument

On November 8, Erskine moved the Court of King's Bench
to set aside the verdict on the ground that the Judge had
misdirected the jury. He was granted a rule to show cause
why there should not be a new trial. At the subsequent
hearing, he addressed the court with the contention that
the defendant had in fact had no trial. He had been found
guilty without any investigation of his guilt and without
any power left to the jury to take notice of his innocence.

In his speech Erskine adopted a different approach
from that used in addressing juries. But he argued at
length for the rights of juries and he revealed deep
learning about the law, making ample use of the
pronouncements of Bracton, Coke, Hale and Blackstone.

He also used an impressive array of cases to support his arguments. The speech, said the ever-admiring Fox, was so luminous and so convincing, that it wanted in opposition not a man but a giant. Certainly there was a magic to Erskine's eloquence.

However, the rule was discharged by a unanimous court with Lord Mansfield arguing the case against Erskine from alternative and more persuasive precedents. Mansfield also took the view that jealousy of leaving the law to the Judges was "puerile rant and declamation", since the Judges were totally independent of Ministers and the King.[8]

Nevertheless, Mr Justice Willes upheld Erskine's argument that upon a plea of not guilty, the jury had the right to examine the innocence of the paper charged as a libel. Upon such examination they might acquit the defendant, even in opposition to the directions of the Judge, without rendering themselves liable to penalties. The verdict could then in no way be set aside by the court. However, he was a minority of one, although eventually the court found the indictment against the Dean to be defective and no further proceedings were taken against him.

Success

On a transcript of the trial belonging to Erskine there was later found in his own handwriting a note[9] to the effect that when he applied to the King's Bench for a new trial he had had no hope of success but merely a fixed

---

8.   21 *State Trials*. 1040.
9.   Campbell. *Op.cit.* 433.

resolution to excite the attention of the public and Parliament to the need to amend the law in favour of national freedom. As it happens his wish was fulfilled. The Judges had decided against him but his arguments were a death-blow to their doctrine. Countrywide agitation quickly led to the success of the Libel Bill originally prepared by Erskine and moved in the House of Commons in 1792 by Charles James Fox with its author seconding. It had, in fact, previously been kept in limbo by the House of Lords for eight years.

The Bill became known to future generations as Fox's Libel Act and fully established the right of juries to decide as a matter of law whether or not a writing was libel and not merely that it had been published. It was enacted despite all the Judges in the House of Lords giving an opinion that the Bill was inconsistent with the common law.

Indeed, Lord Chancellor Thurlow, predicting that it would mean the destruction of the law of England, even endeavoured to secure an amendment whereby the court would have been able to grant a new trial if dissatisfied with an acquittal by the jury. This might have brought his prophecy to fruition. No wonder Lord John Campbell wrote that without the invaluable assistance of Erskine as counsel for the Dean of St Asaph the Star Chamber might have been re-established in England.[10]

---

10.   *Ibid.* 435.

CHAPTER 5

Whig Politics and Ill-Humour

Member for Portsmouth

Coming from a Whig family, Erskine was on terms of close friendship with the main Whig leaders of the day, Charles James Fox, Edmund Burke and Richard Brinsley Sheridan.

Fox, one of the great men of his age, was the scourge of Tory governments with his scorn, wit, irony and passionate emotion for the truth. He was one of the best-loved statesmen and orators in English history, held in deep affection and even idolized for his simplicity and common touch in spite of his colourful and not entirely reputable life-style. He was the epitome of the progressive Whig immortalized by Macaulay.

His failure to achieve power, except for short periods, in place of the ice-cold Pitt was a consequence of the bitter hostility towards him of George III and the reaction in England to the French Revolution. Clearly Pitt, and more particularly his father, Lord Chatham, also had high qualities of leadership. But they are not of direct concern in the story of Erskine where at least Pitt the Younger's shortcomings are more in evidence.

Burke, a disciple of Fox and an outstanding philosopher-politician, enjoyed the credit of leading the opposition in the House of Commons to Britain's role in the American War of Independence, both the outbreak and end of which were caused by the ignorance and greed of the King and his weak-willed and subservient Ministers. And Sheridan, the author of *The Rivals* and *The School for Scandal,* excited the imagination with his wit and his fierce spirit of attack against Pitt and his friends.

In view of Erskine's early success at the Bar it is not surprising that these statesmen should see his potential as a valuable ally in St Stephen's Hall where the House of Commons sat. Accordingly, when the Whigs joined the Fox-North coalition government in March 1782 they were quick to create a vacancy at Portsmouth in order to bring Erskine into Parliament. This was done, none too subtly, by inducing the sitting Member, Sir William Gordon, to take the Chiltern Hundreds in exchange for a pension of £1,000 a year. As a consequence Erskine was duly elected to sit for the naval constituency.

Erskine v. Pitt

Expectations of the famous lawyer were high and sparkling debates were anticipated between him and Pitt. But his maiden speech in support of the India Bill, which was intended to secure greater government control over the East India Company, set the tone for many of his parliamentary performances and was regarded as a damp squib. The bewitching effect on juries of his speeches in court was lacking and it became clear that he did not have the same powers of persuasion when addressing fellow MPs. Perhaps it is not surprising since jurors are expected to start with open and attentive minds whereas MPs are a promiscuous audience more impatient of argument and anxious to express their already held views.

As Lord Brougham, whose experience was the other way, put it later, "the Bar was Erskine's stage where he shone alone, and without a rival; it was in the Forum and not the Senate that this great man was seen in his element and in his glory".[1]

Nevertheless, since it was his maiden speech it may be that on this occasion Erskine was paralysed by the conduct of his antagonist. It appears that Pitt fully intended to reply to the newcomer and sat with pen and paper in hand ready to make notes. As Erskine proceeded, however, Pitt's attention wandered and his face began to take on a look of contempt. Eventually, with all eyes upon him he struck the pen through the paper and flung them to the floor. Erskine faltered, and struggled through the remainder of his speech clearly dispirited.[2]

In fact, Pitt had found some reason to dislike Erskine when he was junior to him at the Bar and was always to enjoy unsettling him in the House of Commons. Of course, they were political opponents, both full of ambition and both outstanding speakers. But it remains true that Erskine very rarely shone in parliamentary debate where his usual rapier thrusts turned wooden. It seems likely that, as the *Gentleman's Magazine* put it, "He was overpowered by the commanding tone, the sarcastic

---

1. *Historical Sketches of Statesmen who Flourished in the Time of George III.* 1st Series. 236/7. 1839.
2. Rev. George Croly. *Life of George IV in A History of English Kings.* 1830.

invective, and the cutting irony of Pitt".[3] According to the Duke of Wellington, in military style Pitt managed Erskine by "the ascendancy of terror".

Speaking in the Commons later, Edmund Burke observed that, "The Bar was the scene of his wealth, of his reputation, of his fame; this House was only the scene of his duty ... This House had only the refuse of the honourable and learned gentleman's abilities; they obtained him solely at second-hand. This was the scene of his duty, the other the scene of his pleasure".[4]

Even Erskine's friend Sheridan was to say to his face at a dinner, "you are afraid of Pitt, and that is the flabby part of your character".[5] Nevertheless, in another age with lesser luminaries than Pitt and Fox in the House of Commons he might not have been so eclipsed as a speaker. James Scarlett, later Lord Abinger, for example, wrote that although he admitted Erskine's success in the House of Commons was not equal to his reputation at the Bar he nevertheless believed that he had very great success. He went on to say, "I have heard him several times when he spoke second only to Pitt and Fox, and commanded the profoundest attention".[6]

Yet even when he had become more experienced in parliamentary debate, Erskine was to say in the House of Lords when opposing the Seditious Meetings Bill, "I despair altogether of making any impression by anything I can say; a feeling which disqualifies me from speaking as I ought. I have been accustomed during the greatest part of my life to be animated by the hope and expectation that I might not be speaking in vain ... I have

---

3.   *Op.cit.*
4.   The Modern Orator. *Chatham, Sheridan and Erskine.* 479. 1845.
5.   George Pellew. *Life of Lord Sidmouth.* 1847.
6.   P.C. Scarlett. *Memoir of Lord Abinger.* 66/7. 1877.

often heard it said, and I believe it to be true, that even the most eloquent man living (how then must I be disabled?) and however deeply impressed with his subject, could scarcely find utterance, if he were to be standing up alone, and speaking only against a wall".[7]

Erskine spoke again on the second reading of the India Bill and this time to better effect when arguing that in governing its territories the East India Company should be subordinate to Parliament. The Bill, which was important to the government and well overdue because of long-standing corruption in the Company, was subsequently defeated in the House of Lords after the King had intervened to say that anyone who voted for the Bill would be his enemy. This brought the coalition ministry to an abrupt end. Erskine now found himself in opposition, with Pitt the Prime Minister.

Fearful that an election would be called which might strengthen Pitt's support in the House of Commons, Erskine attacked him as a man prepared to bend his principles in order to remain in power. The Prime Minister, he said, had gone from supporting liberty into a ridiculous posture. With something of his usual style he continued:

And whoever stands upon secret influence against the confidence of this House will find that his abilities, however great they may be, or may be fancied, instead of being a support and protection to him, will only be like the convulsions of a strong man in the agonies of disease, which exhaust the vital spirit faster than the languishing of debility, and bring on death the sooner. Such, in a few hours, I trust, will be the fate of the

---

7.   40 *Parl.His.* 470. 1795.

right honourable gentleman at the head of the present
government. Indeed, I never compare in my own mind
his first appearance in this House, when under the
banners of my right honourable friend he supported the
genuine cause of liberty, with his present melancholy,
ridiculous situation in it, but I am drawn into an
involuntary parody of the scene of Hamlet and his
mother in the closet.

Here he said:

> Look here upon this picture, and on this:
> See what a grace was seated in his youth,
> His father's fire - the soul of Pitt himself,
> A tongue like his to soften or command,
> A station - like the genius of England
> Now lighted on this top of Freedom's hill;
> A combination and a form indeed,
> Where every god did seem to set his seal
> To give his country earnest of a patriot.

He then added, "Look you what follows":

> Dark, secret influence, like a mildew'd ear,
> Blasting this public virtue: has he eyes!
> Could he this bright assembly leave to please
> To batten on that bench.[8]

How little sting Erskine's words had, however, was seen
some two months later when Pitt deemed that public
support for his government had grown sufficiently to
justify him in dissolving Parliament and calling a General

---

8.   24 *Parl.Hist.* 272. 1784.

Election. Sharing the fate of many of his Whig friends Erskine lost his seat and ceased to represent Portsmouth. He was one of 160 who became known as "Fox's Martyrs".

Spots on the Sun

Now that he was no longer a Member of Parliament, Erskine resumed his appearances as counsel at the bar of the House of Commons. In May 1784 he was instructed on a petition arising out of the election in the City of Westminster. This constituency had a "scot-and-lot" franchise based on the payment of small municipal taxes which unusually gave the vote to the lower middle class and to artisans.

In the 1784 election the Whig candidates, Charles James Fox and Lord Hood, defeated Pitt's nominee. Despite, or because of, the result the government forced a prolonged scrutiny of the votes which prevented Fox from representing Westminster with all its prestige, although he was in the House as Member for a Scottish constituency. Fox accused Pitt of conspiring to injure him but for nine months Pitt ignored his reproach and supported the scrutiny which kept the City of Westminster unrepresented.

However, in the Spring of 1785 the government was defeated on the issue by 162 votes to 124. This ended the scrutiny and Fox and Hood were at last able to take their rightful seats. The House, despite its majority of Pitt supporters, had found the Prime Minister guilty of ungenerous and personal intrigue against an opponent.

It is this background that must explain Erskine's outspoken and disrespectful language to the Commons. Cross-examining a witness who had suggested misconduct by the agents of Fox he asked why the witness assumed that the persons concerned were Mr Fox's agents? When he received the reply that they appeared to be his friends, Erskine retorted, "If all Mr Fox's friends are to be taken to be his agents, every honest man may be so esteemed who is not a Member of this House".

The Speaker ordered Erskine to withdraw the remark and a vote of censure upon him was moved. Whilst considering his reply Erskine was pained to hear Pitt contemptuously remark that it was not worth their while to take any notice of the language of the learned gentleman as it probably formed part of his instructions!

Later, when at the bar of the House on behalf of the East India Company, Erskine denounced the new government's India Bill which had replaced that of his own party as a "vile imposter". On the Speaker again calling him to order, Erskine replied, "If, Mr Speaker, I have been guilty of any irregularity, it arises solely from a diminution of that respect which I was accustomed to feel for this assembly before it was shorn of its dignity - but which no longer animates me". He then continued in ironic tones to taunt the House which he said he supposed was "so pure, so elevated and so wise".

The Speaker once more interrupted him, asking him to confine himself to the matter of the petition. Erskine replied that the hour was too late for the House to consider so important a subject. The Speaker firmly told him that it did not become counsel at the bar to tell the House when it should adjourn and invited him to withdraw altogether if he had nothing further to say on behalf of his client. Erskine thereupon continued his speech but against hostility from both sides of the House.

Discreditable Speech

Yet another display which gave little credit to Erskine's

conduct occurred when he appeared for the Crown in the case of *Rex v. Motherill* at the Sussex Assizes at East Grinstead in March 1786. The accused, who was deformed and of low moral character, was charged with felony in having assaulted a Miss Wade, a young lady between 16 and 17 years of age.

She had been set down by a friend outside her father's door about 10 o'clock one night after returning from a ball. The prisoner, who was loitering nearby, was alleged to have taken her by force to a churchyard where the assault took place.

The defence argued that nothing occurred to which she did not consent. There was strong local prejudice against Motherill, however, since Miss Wade was the daughter of a dignitary of the neighbourhood, and he was not helped by the law of the time which provided that although death was the penalty for felony the prisoner was not permitted to have counsel speak on his behalf.

This bar which put the defence at a serious disadvantage was, of course, no fault of Erskine's. But he did himself address the jury in what may be regarded as an unfortunate manner. Lord John Campbell, who normally sang the praises of Erskine, considered his speech on this occasion to be an harangue which was made the "more objectionable by its affected candour".[9]

After referring to the prisoner as a wicked and unhappy wretch for whom the jury should feel compassion Erskine turned his attention to the young lady. He painted a glowing picture of her beauty and purity but, to explain some inconsistencies in her evidence, insinuated that she was weak in her understanding. And, he professed to believe that because of her beauty even

---

9.   *Op.cit.* 438.

murder was an offence of no great importance when compared with that of which the prisoner was accused.

After a partial sketch of the facts he then concluded with deep and unprofessional irony, saying:

If there is any probability in favour of the prisoner at the bar, in God's name let him have it. But there is no probability in his favour, none that any reasonable mind can for a moment entertain; for, let me ask you this question, whether it be consistent with anything you ever saw, heard, or read of, that a young lady of hitherto chaste and virtuous life, artless, simple, and innocent in her manners, should all of a sudden go out on a tempestuous night - leave her father's house, not to throw herself into the arms of a lover, who had addressed her and endeavoured to seduce her, but into the arms of a stranger, with nothing to recommend him, with nothing on earth to captivate or seduce the fancy?

It is repugnant to reason to believe it - it is a thing incredible, that the most viciously disposed woman could go into the arms of the squalid wretch before you! I do not mean to insult him by the expression; his wickedness renders him an object of compassion. But if he is not to be insulted, a virtuous, innocent, miserable, ruined lady is not to pass unredressed; nor the breach of God's laws and the country's to pass unrevenged ... Justice is all I ask at your hands ... If you can go home tonight, and satisfy yourselves that this young lady either has not been violated in point of fact, or that, having been so, it has been with her own consent; if you can persuade yourselves of that absurd and improbable proposition, after you shall have heard all the evidence, I shall not call your mercy in question; it is a matter which will rest with your own consciences.[10]

What the jury made of this strange speech we do not know. But Motherill was entitled to a fair trial and, after hearing all the evidence, the jury found him, Not Guilty. For once Erskine's address was discreditable and perhaps for that reason he failed to persuade the jury as he did so often on many important issues of liberty.

We know so little of Erskine's personal life that it may be tempting to think that he was suffering from some illness or loss at the time of both this trial and his appearances at the bar of the Commons. It is unlikely that being no longer a Member of Parliament would have affected him deeply since it left him able to concentrate on his lucrative practice at the Bar. However, he had formed lasting friendships with Fox and Sheridan and may have missed working with them at the pinnacle of the political life of the nation. But to offset that he was a great favourite of the Prince of Wales, himself then a Whig, who appointed him to be his Attorney-General.

In any event, he wrote at this time to Lord Auckland, "I continue highly successful in my profession - being now I may say as high as I can go at *the Bar*. The rest depends on politics which at present are adverse. But my ambition is satisfied with my present situation".[11] He made no reference to any illness or loss.

Retirement of the Earl of Mansfield

We next come across Erskine upon the retirement of Lord Mansfield in 1788 after 32 fruitful years as Lord Chief

---

10. *Ibid.* 440.
11. BM. *Add.Mss.* 29,475. fol. 23. (July 16, 1786).

Justice of the King's Bench.

Mansfield was venerated as a Judge by his contemporaries. In the historical *Somersett's Case* in 1771 he had held that a slave once brought into England was a free man or woman. He also allowed Turks, Hindus and other non-Christians to be sworn as witnesses according to the ceremonies of their own religions. And he made governors of English provinces responsible in English courts for wrongful acts committed by them against individuals whilst they were governors.

In his long tenure as Lord Chief Justice he was involved in only two cases in which the whole Bench were not unanimous, and only two of his judgments were reversed on appeal. And, he was completely impartial in the trial of Lord George Gordon after rioters had burnt to the ground his fine house and valuable library in London's Bloomsbury Square.

To some extent, however, he was under the spell of Erskine's advocacy. Sir Nathaniel Wraxall, for example, wrote, "The Earl of Mansfield himself, the Oracle of Themis, before whom every created thing under the roof of Westminster Hall became dumb and submissive ... even he often seemed to shrink from the contest, and gave way to the impetuous flexibility of an individual, who, though sometimes foiled, yet, like Antaeus, derived strength from every fall".[12]

On the retirement being announced the lawyers who practised in the King's Bench asked Erskine to write and present to the Judge an address on their behalf. Eager to do so, Erskine wrote that counsel affectionately assured his Lordship they regretted, "with a just sensibility, the loss of a magistrate whose conspicuous and exalted

---

12. *Historical Memoirs of My Own Time.* 1815.

talents conferred dignity upon the profession, whose enlightened and regular administration of justice made its duties less difficult and laborious, and whose manners rendered them pleasant and respectable".

Whilst the messenger waited Mansfield wrote his reply within five minutes of receiving the letter. He paid tribute to the "learning and candour" of the members of the Bar. And added that "the liberality and integrity of their practice freed the judicial investigation of truth and justice from difficulties".

Mansfield was revered in all common law countries and after his resignation, at the age of 83, he retired to his house at Kenwood where he spent his remaining years in full possession of all his faculties. He died in 1793 and is buried in Westminster Abbey. He was succeeded as Chief Justice by Lord Kenyon, whose intellectual powers did not match those of his predecessor but who had an equally high regard for Erskine's talents.

CHAPTER 6

Freedom of the Press

House of Commons v. Stockdale

In the following year Erskine was to make what Lord John Campbell described as "the finest speech ever delivered at the English Bar; that won a verdict which for ever established the freedom of the press in England".[1] A speech which the *Edinburgh Review* claimed was "justly regarded by all English lawyers as a consummate specimen of the art of addressing a jury - as a standard, a sort of precedent for treating cases of libel".[2]

The case involved was the prosecution of John Stockdale by the House of Commons for an alleged libel upon itself. Ironically, the Motion to prosecute was moved by Erskine's friend and strong advocate of press freedom, Charles James Fox. The trial came on before Lord Kenyon and a Special Jury on December 9, 1789.[3] Special Juries

---

1.   *Op.cit.* 443.
2.   xvi. 109. (1810).
3.   *State Trials.* xxii. 237. 1789.

were composed of 12 "well-born and educated men", normally drawn by the Crown from a special panel of persons with a much higher property qualification than was the case with common jurors. They were often more sympathetic to prosecutors than prisoners and rather surprisingly, they were not abolished until the Juries Act of 1949. What Tom Paine, who experienced them more than once, had to say about them we shall see later.

The background to the case was the dramatic impeachment of Warren Hastings, the former Governor-General of Bengal for high crimes and misdemeanours. Hastings was much admired for having laid the foundations of a vast empire in India, although he had done so with a terrible, ruthless efficiency and extensive plunder. But was he guilty of corruption? Pitt was Prime Minister and was by no means convinced of Hastings' guilt. Yet he left control of the impeachment to an hostile parliamentary Opposition led with passionate eloquence by a partisan Edmund Burke who vowed "immortal hatred" against Hastings.

Burke publicly alleged that Hastings was corrupt, fraudulent, oppressive, wild, savage, unprincipled, "a wild beast who groans in a corner over the dead and dying, a captain-general of iniquity, thief, tyrant robber, cheat, swindler". As Sir James Fitzjames Stephen, the eminent jurist, was to remark, "Burke certainly did not fail in the duty of calling names".[4]

It says something about the morality of the time that, being so biased, Burke was nonetheless entrusted with drawing the articles of Hastings' impeachment. These conspicuously omitted to make specific allegations of crimes and, according to Stephen, they violated all legal

---

4.   *Nuncomar and Impey.* i. 28. 1885.

rules and were "full of invective, oratorical matter, needless recitals, arguments, statements of evidence - everything in fact which can possibly serve to make an accusation difficult to understand and to meet".[5]

In the event, it was only after a seven-year trial before his peers in the House of Lords that Hastings was acquitted on all counts. At the same time, Burke who had become too closely, indeed too personally, involved in his prosecution left the House of Commons for ever.

Impeachment of Warren Hastings

With the commencement of the impeachment proceedings, Burke's inflammatory language against Hastings was repeated in all the newspapers as well as in the House of Lords itself. Furthermore, the Articles of Impeachment which were printed for the record of the House of Commons came to be prematurely sold all over the land creating a strong prejudice against the accused. Disturbed by all this pre-trial abuse, and in the absence of the concept of *sub-judice,* the Rev. Mr Logan, a Minister of the Church of Scotland, wrote a small book, consisting of 110 pages, in defence of Hastings. It must be conceded, however, that in attacking the prosecutors the book bore some of the hallmarks of its principal target, Burke.

The book compared the House of Commons to an inquisition rather than a court of Parliament and, with its own brand of invective and irony, accused those who instigated the impeachment of personal animosity rather than seeking public justice. Of course, there was a great deal of truth in this and it is clear that the author's only

---

5.   *Ibid.* ii. 8/9.

desire was to show Hastings's innocence.

Logan took the book to John Stockdale, a respectable bookseller in Piccadilly, who published it in the usual course of his business. Having an immediate and very extensive sale, the House of Commons directed the Attorney-General, Sir Archibald Macdonald, to file an information for libel against Stockdale.

The evidence against him presented to the jury by the prosecution consisted only of proof of publication since, as seen above, it had earlier been confirmed by Lord Mansfield that whether a work was libellous or not was for the Judge alone to decide. The jury could only consider whether it had been published and the truth or falsity of any innuendoes. In fact, despite the endorsement of the Lord Chief Justice, this rule stemmed originally from the Star Chamber which had enjoyed sole jurisdiction in cases of defamation and which in all cases before it decided both law and fact without a jury.

Since the case was heard before Fox's Libel Act was enacted the Attorney-General unnecessarily introduced the issue of the alleged libel himself and quoted selected passages from the book in an endeavour to prove defamation. In response, Erskine in his address to the jury argued that they should judge the whole book and not just the quoted passages. It had, he said, some 2,530 lines out of which only 40 or 50 from different parts had been artfully put together to give a false impression of the work.

The Attorney-General also deplored what he called the licentiousness of the press and proceeded to inform the jury that, "the liberty of the press consists in its good regulation ... it must be from time to time lopped of its unjust excesses".

In contrast, Erskine put a stark proposition to the jury. He told them that if they thought the book to be the work

of a man with an intelligent mind and compassion for a
fellow man he believed to be innocent but convicted him
nevertheless, they would not only cause an injustice but
would break up the press of England and surrender its
rights and liberties for ever.

Erskine studiously separated his defence of Stockdale
from a defence of Hastings which was not his purpose.
Nonetheless, in an endeavour to excite some compassion
for Hastings and thereby the author who defended him,
he drew the following colourful picture of the
impeachment which was proceeding before the House of
Lords:

There the most august and striking spectacle was daily
exhibited, which the world ever witnessed. A vast stage
of justice was erected, awful from its high authority,
splendid from its illustrious dignity, venerable from the
learning and wisdom of its Judges, captivating and
affecting from the mighty concourse of all ranks and
conditions which daily flocked into it, as into a theatre
of pleasure; there, when the whole public mind was at
once awed and softened to the impression of every
human affection, there appeared, day after day, one
after another, men of the most powerful and exalted
talents, eclipsing by their accusing eloquence the most
boasted harangues of antiquity; rousing the pride of
national resentment by the boldest invectives against
broken faith and violated treaties, and shaking the
bosom with alternate pity and horror by the most
glowing pictures of insulted nature and humanity; ever
animated and energetic, from the love of fame, which
is the inherent passion of genius; firm and
indefatigable, from a strong prepossession of the justice
of their cause.

Gentlemen, when the author sat down to write the

book now before you, all this terrible, unceasing, exhaustless artillery of warm zeal, matchless vigour of understanding, consuming and devouring eloquence, united with the highest dignity, was daily, and without prospect of conclusion, pouring forth upon one private unprotected man, who was bound to hear it, in the face of the whole people of England, with reverential submission and silence ... When it is remembered that we are not angels, but weak fallible men, and that even the noble Judges of that high tribunal are clothed beneath their ermines with the common infirmities of man's nature, it will bring us all to a proper temper for considering the book itself.

If, Erskine went on to say, Mr Hastings was entitled to write such a book in his own defence, as he was, then it was proper and could not be a crime for Mr Logan to do so for him. It could not be endured that Hastings should suffer without being permitted to have something submitted to the judgment of mankind in his defence. If that were the law (which it was for the jury to decide) then he would have no trial, "that great hall, built by our fathers for English justice, is no longer a court, but an altar; and an Englishman, instead of being judged in it by *God and his Country* is a *Victim and a Sacrifice*".

Erskine promised the jury that he would make out to their satisfaction that the book was a *bona fide* defence of Hastings and not a cloak and cover for scandal on the House of Commons. This he proceeded to do with a painstaking examination of it in great detail.

The Indian Chief

Erskine then addressed the jury in what Lord John

Campbell described, with perhaps some hyperbole, as "the finest passage to be found in ancient or modern oratory - for imagery, for passion, for pathos, for variety and beauty of cadence, for the concealment of art, for effect in gaining the object of the orator".[6] At least that judgment may justify quoting from the speech at some length.

> It may, and must be true, Erskine said, that Mr Hastings has repeatedly offended against the rights and privileges of Asiatic government, if he was the faithful deputy of a power which could not maintain itself for an hour without trampling upon both; he may and must have offended against the laws of God and nature, if he was the faithful viceroy of an empire wrested in blood from the people to whom God and nature had given it; he may and must have preserved that unjust dominion over timorous and abject nations by a terrifying, overbearing, insulting superiority, if he was the faithful administrator of your government, which having no root in consent or affection, no foundation in similarities of interests, nor support from any one principle which cements men together in society, could only be upheld by alternate stratagem and force.
>
> The unhappy people of India, feeble and effeminate as they are from the softness of their climate, and subdued and broken as they have been by the knavery and strength of civilization, still occasionally start up in all the vigour and intelligence of insulted nature; to be governed at all, they must be governed with a rod of iron; and our empire in the East would, long since, have been lost to Great Britain, if civil skill and

---

6.   *Op.cit.* 447.

military prowess had not united their efforts to support
an authority - which Heaven never gave, by means
which it never can sanction.

Gentlemen, I think I can observe that you are
touched with this way of considering the subject; and
I can account for it. I have not been considering it
through the cold medium of books, but have been
speaking of man and his nature, and of human
dominion, from what I have seen of them myself
amongst reluctant nations submitting to our authority.
I know what they feel, and how such feelings can alone
be repressed. I have heard them in my youth from a
naked savage, in the indignant character of a prince
surrounded by his subjects, addressing the Governor
of a British colony, holding a bundle of sticks in his
hand, as the notes of his unlettered eloquence: "Who
is it"? said the jealous ruler over the desert, encroached
upon by the restless foot of English adventure - "who
is it that causes this river to rise in the high
mountains, and to empty itself into the ocean? Who is
it that causes to blow the loud winds of winter, and
that calms them again in the summer? Who is it that
rears up the shade of those lofty forests, and blasts
them with the quick lightning at his pleasure? The
same Being who gave to you a country on the other
side of the waters, and gave ours to us; and by this
title we will defend it", said the warrior, throwing
down his tomahawk upon the ground, and raising the
war-sound of his nation.

These are the feelings of subjugated man all round
the globe; and depend upon it, nothing but fear will
control where it is vain to look for affection ... it might
be better perhaps to think of perpetually securing
[justice] by recalling our troops and our merchants, and
abandoning our oriental empire. Until this be done,

neither religion nor philosophy can be pressed very far into the aid of reformation and punishment. If England, from a lust of ambition and dominion, will insist on maintaining despotic rule over distant and hostile nations, and gives commission to her viceroys to govern them with no other instructions than to preserve them, and to secure permanently their revenues; with what colour of consistency or reason can she place herself in the moral chair, and affect to be shocked at the execution of her own orders; adverting to the exact measure of wickedness and injustice necessary to their execution, and complaining only of the *excess* as the immorality, considering her authority as a dispensation for breaking the commands of God, and the breach of them as only punishable when contrary to the ordinances of man.

Reverting to the book, Erskine continued that he was against punishing strong opinions which might be expressed with no evil intent when a writer warmed to his subject. Otherwise minds would be silenced by the terrors of punishment and this would deny the people works of genius that could expand the boundaries of human reason.

Under such terrors, he said, all the great lights of science and civilization would be extinguished. Men would be unable to communicate their free thoughts to one another if a lash were held over them. It was the nature of all things that were great and useful to be wild and irregular. We had to accept them with their alloys, or live without them. "Tempests occasionally shake our dwellings and dissipate our commerce, but they scourge before them the lazy elements which without them would stagnate into pestilence".

In the same way, liberty had to be taken as it was. It

might be reduced to regularity and be shaped into a perfect model of severe law. But it would then not be liberty and we would die under the lash of such unyielding injustice which had been taken in exchange for freedom.

Towards the end of his speech Erskine expressed the hope that he had performed his duty to his client. He had been urged on, he told the jury, by his love of justice, and the country's Constitution which was the inheritance of the world. These were the motives which had animated him in defence of a person who was a stranger to him and whose shop he had never entered. They might not be relevant in cases involving property or unjust libels. But in this case they were when the issue involved was not a question of law but a pure question of fact.

Gift of Persuasion

After Erskine had concluded his speech, the Attorney-General felt obliged to say to the jury in a fine tribute to his opponent, "My learned friend and I stand very much contrasted with each other in this case. To him belong infinite eloquence and ingenuity, a gift of persuasion beyond that which I almost ever knew fall to any man's share, and a power of language greater than that which ever met my ear".

Lord Chief Baron Abinger, formerly James Scarlett, who was present in court, described to Lord Campbell the effect of the speech on those present. "They all actually believed", he said, "that they saw before them the Indian chief with his bundle of sticks and his tomahawk. Their breasts thrilled with the notes of his unlettered eloquence, and they thought they heard him raise the war-sound of his nation".[7]

Lord Brougham later wrote that there were no finer things in modern, and few finer in ancient eloquence than the celebrated passage of the Indian chief. Nor had beautiful language ever been used with more curious felicity to raise a striking and appropriate image before the mind than in the simile of the winds "lashing before them the lazy elements, without which the tempest would stagnate into pestilence".[8]

Such are the impressions we cannot absorb merely by reading the speech. We cannot hear or see what *The Edinburgh Review* described as, "the witchery of this extraordinary man's voice, eye and action".[9]

And Brougham went on to describe Erskine's voice as of surpassing sweetness, clear, flexible, strong, earnest and free from harshness or monotony. Juries had declared, he said, that they felt it impossible to remove their eyes from him when he had riveted and fascinated them by his first glance. He had a thorough knowledge of men, their passions and feelings. He was lively and brilliant. "He knew every avenue to the heart, and could at will make all its chords vibrate to his touch".[10]

It is worthy of note that Brougham consciously attempted to emulate Erskine as a barrister but did not always exhibit the required application or eloquence. In view of Erskine's popular success, on two occasions Brougham reviewed some of his published speeches in order to bring himself to public notice as a young MP. In this he succeeded.

All these remarkable tributes to Erskine were richly

---

7.   Campbell. *Op.cit.* 450.
8.   *Historical Sketches. Op.cit.* 242.
9.   *Op.cit.* 114.
10.   *Op.cit.* 237/8.

deserved. Further, we should also observe that in an age when democracy was widely derided, and exploitation regarded as normal, Erskine in his speech exposed the raw nerve of colonial rule. In excusing Hastings personally from the charge of corruption, he nevertheless revealed the inhumanity involved for millions of people in the strategy which Hastings was charged to put into effect. In doing so he exhibited a sensibility towards human beings, subjected to indignity, loss of freedom and often death far away by policy dictated from home, that was not always perceived by his contemporary admirers.

To return to the trial. Lord Kenyon, in his summing up to the jury, placed no stress upon the role of the Judge in determining whether there was a libel, and said they had to decide two issues; did the defendant publish - which was admitted - and was there a libel on the House of Commons.

Whilst the good part of the book would not sanctify a bad part the jury had the right to look at all the context and the book as a whole.

After retiring for two hours, the jury returned a verdict of Not Guilty against John Stockdale, and Erskine had triumphed again.

Private View

Warren Hastings had wished to retain Erskine as his counsel. However, his impeachment was instigated by the Whig leaders and Erskine declined with great reluctance, saying that in court he could have smitten Burke "hip and thigh". He told the jury, however, that he was pleased to have the trust and confidence of Stockdale who knew of his personal friendship with those whom Logan had attacked in his book.

It is interesting that Erskine never even met Hastings. He had, in fact, been given an opportunity to do so earlier, in 1786, at the invitation of the Bishop of St Asaph and Dr Shipley. But in a letter to the Bishop, Erskine regretted that illness prevented him from attending at the Bishop's palace when Hastings would be present. He then revealed what his instincts were, some three years before being briefed in the Stockdale case.

After making his apologies he wrote, "Although he [Hastings] is prosecuted by a person I love and respect" [Burke] "I should have been happy in an opportunity of showing him that an English lawyer does not conclude that a man is guilty of crimes, because he is prosecuted for them, and that it is not the genius of this Constitution to try men for their [a word author cannot decipher in Erskine's manuscript letter] Liberties and properties in assemblies not competent from their very constitution to the administration of private Justice".

He indicated that he considered Hastings may have committed an error of judgment in his administration of public affairs but was not guilty of corruption. And whereas corruption had to be proved by facts, when an error of judgment was the subject of criminal charges, prejudice, misconception and party interest replaced proof.

Further, he was opposed, he wrote, to impeachment instead of a criminal trial because it did not proceed "on principles of English Justice. [Those involved] were bound by no oaths, limited by no principles of judgment, confined to no Rules of Evidence, and every man's mind made up on the subject".

Erskine concluded his letter on a personal note, saying that his face was so "inflamed and swelled" that it was impossible for him to go out. And, as he had no other nurse or attendant than his wife she desired the Bishop to make her apologies to Dr and Mrs Shipley.[11]

Democrat

Shortly after the Stockdale case, a tired Erskine paid his first visit to Paris where he wished to witness the state of the Revolution. He stayed for a few weeks and on his return expressed his admiration at what he had seen. With some dismay, Samuel Romilly wrote in a letter that Erskine had returned from Paris a "violent democrat" - something of a demon in England at that time, even without the adjective. He had gone so far, Romilly continued, as to have a coat made in the style of the uniform of the Jacobins which he intended to wear in the House of Commons[12] - although he never did so.

11. BM. *Add.Mss.* 29,169. f.6. (1786).
12. *Memoirs.* i. 408. 1840.

CHAPTER 7

Coffee-House Sedition and Return to Parliament

John Frost and "Wretched Vermin"

Some three years later, in 1793, Erskine was briefed to defend attorney John Frost before another Special Jury on a charge of treason in uttering seditious words.[1] In a phrase which echoed the words of "Freeborn John" Lilburne in the seventeenth century, Frost had remarked that he was for equality and no King and in favour of improving the franchise.

Even the Attorney-General in prosecuting, conceded that to espouse the doctrine of "Equality and no King" had long been held not to infringe the right of free speech. But times had changed he argued, and with the French Revolution across the Channel, punishment was now justified. He also accepted, he said, the "great authority" of Mr Justice Foster's ruling that mere words could not be treasonable without overt traitorous acts. However, he

---

1.   *State Trials. Op.cit.* 472.

wanted to extend this judgment by adding the gloss that a great deal depended upon the time and season and whether the accused was a well-disposed person. It might seem from these admissions and special pleading that in law little by way of defence was necessary. But Erskine knew that the French Revolution had produced terror in many hearts, including those of wealthy men who sat on Special Juries. He therefore first established, in cross-examining the prosecution witnesses, that Frost had spoken the words complained of in consequence of provocation after dining and wining perhaps too well in the Percy coffee house in London.

He also produced letters written to Frost by no less than the Prime Minister, William Pitt, clearly revealing that at an earlier time they had been working closely together for the reform of parliamentary representation. Such reform, Pitt had written, was essential for "the independence of Parliament and the liberty of the people". He must now have winced at the resemblance of those words to the sentiments of Erskine.

The prosecution response was that reform being no longer in fashion people who perversely continued to express such views were susceptible to treasonable suggestions that the Constitution be changed by having no King.

As to the French Revolution, which figured so largely in the prosecution case, Erskine told the jury that the good or evil of it belonged to the French people themselves. They had the right, like every other people upon earth, to change their government.

But, apart from that, he said, the essence of the prosecution case against his client was that he could not be afforded the benefit of Mr Justice Foster's ruling unless he could be shown to be "otherwise well disposed". Where then, he asked, was the presumption of innocence?

"Good God, Gentlemen", exclaimed Erskine flinging himself into a diplomatic fury, "Are we in an English Court of Justice? Are we sitting in judgment before the Chief Justice of England, with the assistance of a jury of Englishmen. And am I in such a presence to be called upon to prove the good disposition of my client before I can be entitled to those rules of evidence which apply equally to the just and the unjust, and by which an evil disposition must be proved before it shall even be suspected?"

Tainted Witnesses

Referring to the witnesses against Frost who had initiated the prosecution, Erskine spoke to the jury of the government's use of well-paid spies and informers. Of its hiring defamation and "stabbing in the dark by anonymous accusations" eminent and virtuous men who were portrayed as cuthroats fermenting sedition. To *The Edinburgh Review* such spies were "wretched vermin".[2]

For Erskine, society was under the lash of such informers bent on hunting men in the privacy of their domestic lives. Had an English gentleman, he asked, now to fill his glass of wine by a measure, lest, believing his neighbours were joining with him in happy relaxation and freedom of thought, he should find his character blasted and himself in prison?

"Such a vexatious system of inquisition", Erskine said, "the disturber of household peace, began and ended with the Star Chamber; the venerable law of England never knew it; her noble, dignified, and humane policy soars

---

2.   *Op.cit.* 19.

above the little irregularities of our lives, and disdains to enter our closets without a warrant founded upon complaint".

Although Erskine called no witnesses, since the words were not denied, the Attorney-General insisted on his right of reply to the jury who, after retiring for an hour-and-a-half, found Frost, Guilty. His life was then ruined by his being struck off the roll of attorneys, placed in the pillory at Charing Cross and imprisoned in the plague-ridden Newgate gaol for six months.

It was one of Erskine's rare failures but, no doubt, the Special Jury were influenced by reports of the atrocities in France. However, Erskine was correct in his interpretation of the law and he won the cheers of the crowds outside the court. And when Frost was released from prison after serving his sentence, he was carried along the streets by the multitude shouting with joy at his freedom. Eventually he received a royal pardon from the Prince Regent in 1813, although his name was not restored to the roll.

Parliament and Fox's Libel Act

In the autumn of 1790 Erskine had been returned again to the House of Commons for Portsmouth. By now he was estranged from Burke who had moved away from the Foxites during the course of a split in the ranks of the Whigs. Perhaps for that reason, Erskine argued in the House that the recent dissolution of Parliament had brought to an end the impeachment of Hastings. This was not the constitutional position, however, and his long speech, in the course of which he broke down from fatigue, was not well received.

A furious Burke rose to ask if those whose ideas never

travelled beyond a *nisi prius* case (ie, a trial by a jury before a single Judge) were better qualified to judge what ought to be the length of an impeachment, than a rabbit who bred six times a year was able to judge of the proper time for the gestation of an elephant. Continuing the assault on Erskine, he then claimed that lawyers in the House of Commons were mere birds of passage perched there for a later flight to the House of Lords.

Erskine calmly replied that if that were true of him he would hardly have landed on the naked bough which supported him when the luxurious foliage on the other side of the House would have afforded him shelter and accelerated his flight.

Nonetheless, Erskine's position on the impeachment was also contrary to the stand taken by his party and he received little support. His passing remark that the country should be governed by law was greeted with a retort by Burke that he would be pleased to see the country governed by law but not by lawyers.

On the instigation of Erskine, in May, 1792 Fox introduced into the House a Motion for leave to bring in his Bill to enable the jury, and not the Judge, to decide generally on the merits of the case in prosecutions for libel. As seen above, Erskine had helped materially in drafting the Bill which declared the principles he had advocated in the courts. Accordingly there were great expectations when he rose to second the Motion. These were deflated, however, when he himself observed that he had nothing new to bring forward on the subject having said it all before to juries. Despite this he unwisely spoke at length and seems to have offended the House by bringing his professional character to the fore and exhibiting some vanity. It was perhaps excusable after his exertions and enterprise in the cause but revealed a lack of judgment. Nevertheless, as we have seen, Fox's Libel

Act became law with beneficial results.

Horrors of War

The progress of the French Revolution was now having an even deeper impression in England. When it had commenced many in this country believed with Wordsworth that an evil despotism had been overthrown and that France was heading for a constitutional monarchy similar to our own. However, with the execution of Louis XVI sympathy gave way to intense hostility and one consequence was a deepening of the schism in the ranks of the Whigs.

Whilst many politicians feared the idea of a republic spreading across the Channel, Erskine continued to forecast that the Revolution would lead to general liberty. As a result, remaining allied with Fox, he forfeited the pleasure of his patron, the Prince of Wales. At the same time Pitt's government entered upon its period of repression to counter what it saw as a danger of Jacobinism growing in Britain. This involved the enactment of new penal laws which Erskine courageously opposed.

He considered the issue was whether the Constitution could be preserved by coercion, or would be better served by the impulse of its own spirit and its own principles. Whether to create disaffection in the people or encourage them by granting them fair representation in Parliament.

He also continued to urge that the government should keep up friendly relations with the French Republic in an endeavour to avoid war. To this end he later reminded MPs of the horrors of war and the suffering it caused to the country's soldiers and sailors.

The life of a modern soldier, he said, is ill represented
by heroic fiction. War has means of destruction more
formidable than the cannon and the sword. Of the
thousands and tens of thousands who perished in our
late contests with France and Spain a very small part
ever felt the stroke of an enemy; the rest languished
in tents and ships, amidst damps and putrefaction -
pale, torpid, spiritless, and helpless - gasping and
groaning, unpitied among men, made obdurate by long
continuance of hopeless misery; and were at last
whelmed into pits, or heaved into the ocean, without
notice, without remembrance. Thus, by incommodious
encampments and unwholesome stations, where
courage is useless and enterprise impracticable, fleets
are silently dispeopled, and armies sluggishly melt
away.[3]

At this time a number of Correspondence Societies were
forming throughout the country to campaign for
parliamentary reform and peace, causes which Pitt and
other earlier supporters of these aims now perceived as
a terrible threat. The government urged magistrates to
take severe action against such societies and their
members whenever possible.

Political associations were forbidden, meetings broken
up and opponents of the government branded as public
enemies. Erskine asked what circumstances called for
such extraordinary measures? What could justify reducing
or endangering freedom and weakening public liberty?
Why, he questioned, should opponents of government
policy suffer suspicions of treason and rebellion?

Indeed, he made another speech in the House of

---

3.   80 *Parl.Hist.* 97. 1795.

Commons calling for parliamentary reform but, in the temper of the times, the Motion secured only 41 votes against 282. But he did not merely speak out. True to his beliefs and at risk to his public prestige he also joined both the Society of Friends of Liberty and the Society of Friends of the People for Advocating Parliamentary Reform.

CHAPTER 8

Fear of Revolution

Tom Paine's "Rights of Man"

As we have seen, in the early 1780s the thoughts of some leading statesmen, including Pitt, had turned towards parliamentary reform. Indeed, Pitt actually advocated such reform in his maiden speech to the House of Commons in 1781. To do so was not in accord with precedent for a new Member but perhaps it was not surprising after the country's double misfortune of nearly a century of rule by oligarchs and now with a King demanding a return to rule by divine right.

Moreover, the government of an atavistic King and an unreformed Parliament soon brought upon itself a severe reverse with the victory of the American colonists in 1782. It then suffered a further check from "Grattan's Revolution" in Ireland in 1782/3 which achieved independence and an Irish Parliament for 19 years.

Both these Revolutions enjoyed the sympathy of large sections of the British people including the manufacturing middle class and the artisans and craftsmen of the cities. Then, with the advent of the French Revolution Pitt began to fear that a similar sentiment of *lese-majeste* in Britain might spread the contagion in France across the Channel. Also to swing round in his allegiance, although not his conservative philosophy, was Edmund Burke who sounded the alarm with his *Reflections on the French Revolution*, published in 1790, and his ill-fated rejection of the rights of the "swinish multitude".

Under the legend of "Church and King", mobs were now being raised to attack the homes of leading sympathizers with the early stages of the French Revolution. Included was the house of Joseph Priestley. A Unitarian scientist who discovered oxygen and several other gases, Priestley owned perhaps the best equipped laboratory in the country which was now destroyed by such a mob. Inflamed by their wrecking activities, they finally broke Priestley's wine bottles, flooded his cellar and drank themselves silly. Insensible though they were, they then managed to set the house on fire. The shabby reaction at the summit of society is revealing. "I am not sorry", wrote the Marquis of Buckingham. Not to be outdone, the King told Home Secretary, Henry Dundas, "I cannot but feel better pleased that Priestley is the sufferer".

Seditious Libel

Not surprisingly against this background, in 1792 the government decided to prosecute Thomas Paine for seditious libel in Part II of his *Rights of Man*. Indeed, this prosecution marked the commencement of the serious targeted repression of radical opinion. When Pitt's niece quoted the book to him, the Prime Minister revealingly replied, "Paine is no fool, he is perhaps right; but if I did what he wants, I should have thousands of bandits on my hands tomorrow, and London burnt".[1] In fact, Pitt's imagination already saw thousands of bandits everywhere.

Thomas Paine, who was born at Thetford in Norfolk in 1737, had emigrated to America where his pamphlets *Common Sense* and *The American Crisis* had stiffened the resolve of George Washington's army at crucial moments in the war and led to Paine's closeness to Washington and Jefferson. In the light of his experiences, and having returned to England by 1790, Paine quickly decided to write a rejoinder to Burke.

Part 1 of *The Rights of Man* then appeared in 1791 as a challenge to Burke's *Reflections*. Burke, rather foolishly for a political philosopher, had argued that the Settlement of 1689 had established the form of the English Constitution "for ever". Paine pointedly retorted that the legislators might as well have passed an Act to enable themselves to live for ever. Although Part 1 of the *Rights of Man* enjoyed a wide sale it attracted no attention at all from the government.

Part II, however, made a different impact. This turned to a declaration of positive projects of social reform, in the course of which Paine was critical of the monarchy and the aristocracy. It sold over a million and a half copies - a colossal figure for the time. This galvanized the government into action. The militias were mobilized, justices were told to seek out all distributors of seditious writings and the Attorney-General, Sir Archibald Macdonald, instituted the proceedings against Paine.

The charge of seditious libel was meant to be preliminary to a charge of high treason and Paine's friend, the poet William Blake, convinced him that he was

---

1.   J.R. Green. *Op.cit.* 819.

as good as dead if he did not go at once to Paris where, with others including Jeremy Bentham, he had been elected to the National Convention. It is of interest to note that during the trial the Judge did mistakenly assert that the prisoner was charged with treason.

Paine removed himself to France accordingly and the trial was held *in absentia* in the King's Bench before Lord Chief Justice Kenyon and a Special Jury on December 18, 1792.[2] Despite the incredible sales of his book, however, the feeling against Paine was so strong in some classes of society that even in 1810 the editor of *Erskine's Speeches to Juries,* James Ridgway, unusually set out the whole of the Information against Paine. He also studiously avoided printing parts of a letter Paine had written to the Attorney-General, even though they were put in evidence by the Crown.

Clamour Against Erskine

Erskine received a brief to act for Paine. Thinking that he might soon be appointed Lord Chancellor several of Erskine's friends urged him to refuse the retainer. And when he was walking on Hampstead Heath one dark November evening he was sought out by Lord Loughborough who ominously exclaimed, "Erskine, you must not take Paine's brief", to which Erskine replied, "But I have been retained, and I will take it, by God".

He received a similar message from the Prince of Wales but would not change his mind in spite of a threat that he would be dismissed from his position as the Prince's legal adviser. Although his stand was scrupulously in

---

2.   *State Trials. Op.cit.* 358.

accord with professional etiquette he was widely condemned and became the object of unpleasant attacks in government newspapers.

The Attorney-General, in opening the case, adopted a tone of utmost outrage that such a book should be forced, as he put it, on that part of the public whose minds, he said, were not familiar with its subject-matter. Yet he had already complained of its staggering sale, which could hardly have been enforced.

Explicitly evoking treason, which was not the charge, he also made the preposterous claim that to write that the people did not already have all the rights they needed was in effect levying war upon the King and the Constitution. On the contrary, replied Erskine holding to the point, Fox's Libel Act showed that a published work genuinely written with the object of benefiting mankind could never be a libel, let alone treason.

Erskine asked the court not to allow the prosecution to introduce the letter Paine was alleged to have written to the Attorney-General from Paris since it had nothing to do with the book on which the charge was based. If it were libellous, he said, it could form the basis of another charge; in this case it would be purely prejudicial. Indeed, in the letter Paine not only acknowledged his authorship of *The Rights of Man* but also made a swingeing attack on the King and the Prince of Wales which undoubtedly did produce the prejudice his counsel feared.

On his request being refused, Erskine told the jury that if the Attorney-General was painfully embarrassed for the King by the letter, as he claimed to be, they might inquire what his own embarrassment might be. The Attorney-General felt for the august character of the King, but he (Erskine) stood in the same relation, as Attorney-General, to the Prince of Wales who had been even more bitterly attacked in the letter.

He then referred to the "calumnious clamour" raised against him. "For what"? he asked. "Only for not having shrunk from the discharge of a duty with no personal advantage, only a thousand difficulties". Little indeed did his critics know him, he said, if they thought such attacks would influence his conduct.

In a brilliant exposition of the principles involved, he said,

> I will for ever, at all hazards, assert the dignity, independence and integrity of the English Bar, without which impartial justice, the most valuable part of the English Constitution, can have no existence. From the moment that any advocate can be permitted to say that he will, or will not, stand between the Crown and the subject arraigned in the court where he daily sits to practise, from that moment the liberties of England are at an end. If the advocate refuses to defend, from what he may think of the charge or of the defence, he assumes the character of the Judge; nay, he assumes it before the hour of judgment; and, in proportion to his rank and reputation, puts the heavy influence of, perhaps, a mistaken opinion into the scale against the accused, in whose favour the benevolent principle of English law makes all presumptions ...

In Part II of his book, written as it was some 200 years ago, Paine proclaimed the need for universal public education, for children's allowances and old age pensions, for the public provision of work at wages for the unemployed, and for the financing of these measures with a progressive income tax. Little wonder that the government of the day was filled with dismay.

"When it can be said", Paine wrote, "by any country in the world, 'My poor are happy: neither ignorance nor

distress is to be found among them: my jails are empty
of prisoners, my streets of beggars: the aged are not in
want: the taxes are not oppressive'; when these things can
be said, then may that country boast its Constitution and
its government".[3]

Free Discussion

In his defence of Paine, Erskine explained to the jury how
he saw the limits of free discussion on political matters.
Enjoying the liberty of the press, every man might
address himself critically on the subjects of government
and the Constitution. This included pointing out their
errors and defects, provided he did not intend to deceive
but only sought to enlighten others, however erroneously.
It would be different if he wickedly wrote what he did not
think in order to excite acts of misconduct.

　　If, he continued, in the progress of the human mind no
man could have awakened the public to errors and abuses
in government, how could government have progressed,
through reformation and revolution, from barbarism to
such a pitch of happiness and perfection that the
Attorney-General considered it profane to touch it further
or look for any future improvement?

　　The Attorney-General himself, Erskine reminded the
jury, had admitted that he had not prosecuted the first
part of the book because it circulated only amongst the
"judicious part" of the public. Part II was different,
however, because it had been circulated into every corner
of society. But, Erskine urged, that was not the test. The
test was whether Paine had dealt with only what

3.　　*Rights of Man.* Part II. Thinker's Library. 245. 1944.

appeared to *him* (though it might not to the jury) to be the interest and happiness of England. On this point the book spoke for itself. The principle which pervaded it was that even a bad law should be obeyed until repealed. Otherwise, Paine had said, his disobedience of a law from thinking it bad, might be used to justify another man in disobedience of a good law.

Erskine argued, "Paine insists that English liberty was obtained from usurped power by the struggles of the people. So too say I ... was there any freedom after the original conquest by the Normans? Was not Magna Carta wrested from John by *open force of arms* at Runnymede? ... Were not its stipulations broken, and two and 40 times re-enacted by Parliament, upon the firm demand of the people in the following reigns? I protest it fills me with astonishment to hear these truths brought in question".

The Star Chamber, he continued, had restricted the press of England so that no one could legally write without permission of the state. But truth and freedom found their way with greater force through secret channels; and, unwarned by a free press, Charles was brought to an ignominious death. Cromwell pursued the same system of restraint in support of his government, and the end of it speedily followed. At the restoration of Charles II, the Star Chamber ordinance of 1637 was made into an Act of Parliament, and was followed by the most sanguinary prosecutions which hastened the Glorious Revolution.

Then, these cobwebs were all brushed away. The freedom of the press was restored and history showed that in proportion as the press was free, English government had been secure. Paine's *opinions* were adverse to the system but "I maintain", stressed Erskine, "that *opinion* is free and that *conduct* alone is amenable to the law".

Erskine then told the jury that their jurisdiction to decide whether there was a libel or not was less than a year old. He himself had maintained that the right had long existed but, in any event, it had now been confirmed by an almost unanimous vote of Parliament. In effect he argued that:

1. Fox's Libel Act defined libel as publishing certain kinds of writing from a bad motive.
2. A man who published what he genuinely believed to be true in order to benefit mankind could not be acting from a bad motive.
3. Therefore, published opinions were not criminal unless the publisher wished to injure mankind.
4. On this basis Paine could not possibly be guilty.

Notwithstanding the power of Erskine's pleas, the Special Jury selected by the Crown lawyers, in an astonishing scene, found Paine guilty before the Attorney-General had even replied to Erskine or the Judge had an opportunity to sum up the case! *The Rights of Man* was accordingly condemned as a seditious libel and Paine was sentenced to the medieval punishment of outlawry by which his property was forfeit and he was to be executed if he returned to England.

Prosecutions were now launched against printers, publishers and booksellers throughout the land. The interest of Pitt and his friends in political reform had come to an abrupt end. Instead, retrenchment and repression became the order of the day. At this stage, so far as the criminal law is concerned the Enlightenment had made little impact in England and the King and his government were anxious to keep a tight grip on society for the next two or three decades.

Conspiracy Against Paine

Another consequence of the trial was that Erskine was deprived of his position as Attorney-General to the Prince of Wales in accordance with the threat made earlier. Later, in the trial of John Horne Tooke, Erskine asserted that there had been a conspiracy to prevent Paine being defended. He was to be denied counsel and he (Erskine) was threatened with the loss of office if he appeared as his advocate. "I was told in plain terms", he said, "that I must not defend Mr Paine. I did defend him, and I did lose my office".

Shortly before his death, Erskine reverted to the matter in a letter to Thomas Howell, editor of the *State Trials*. After setting out the background he wrote that he was told that to defend Paine was incompatible with his continuing to be the Prince's Attorney-General.

The Prince himself, he continued, in the most friendly manner acquainted me that it was highly displeasing to the King, and that I ought to endeavour to explain my conduct, which I immediately did in a letter to his Majesty himself, in which, after expressing my sincere attachment to his person, and to the Constitution of the Kingdom, attacked in the work which was to be defended, I took the liberty to claim, as an invaluable part of that very Constitution, the unquestionable right of the subject to make his defence by any counsel of his own free choice, if not previously retained or engaged by office from the Crown; and that there was no other way of deciding whether that was or was not my own situation as Attorney General to the Prince, than by referring, according to custom, that question to the Bar, which I was perfectly willing, and even desirous to do.

In a few days afterwards I received a most gracious message from the Prince, expressing his deep regret in feeling himself obliged to receive my resignation, which was accordingly sent. But I owe it to his Royal Highness to express my opinion, that, circumstanced as he was, he had no other course to take in those disgraceful and disgusting times, and that my retainer for Paine was made a pretext by the King's Ministers for my removal ...

Erskine went on to add that a few years later the Prince, when Regent, sent for him and said that he had no understanding of retainers and was convinced that in defending Paine Erskine had acted from the purest motives. He thereupon appointed him as his Chancellor of the Duchy of Cornwall.[4]

Rex v. Morning Chronicle

The following year saw three more supporters of parliamentary reform prosecuted for seditious libel.[5] This time it was John Lambert, James Parry and James Gray, the proprietors of the respectable *Morning Chronicle*. Their "crime" was to have accepted for publication an address of a society for political information in Derby which complained about the state of the representation of the people.

As this was another of the earliest trials for libel since the enactment of Fox's Libel Act, Erskine told the jury that no one should now contend, as the Attorney-General

---

4.　　Howell's *State Trials*. xxvi. 715.
5.　　*Ibid.* xxii. 954.

had just done, that the "crime" in such a case was an inference of law from the fact. On the contrary, he said, as one of the authors of the Act he could tell them that it involved the law and the fact together. It obliged the jury to find in this alleged crime, as in all others, by extrinsic as well as intrinsic means, the mind and intention with which the fact was committed. The jury, he explained, were the sole arbitrators in the case.

Erskine gave homicide as an example of the need to inquire into intention. Two men, for instance, were together and one of them was killed by the other. It was not an inference in law from the fact of the killing that the person who killed was guilty of murder - it might be manslaughter, justifiable homicide, chance-medley, or it might be murder. The fact did not infer the crime. It was the intention with which the act was committed that was paramount, and this the jury were duty bound to discover and decide upon from all the available evidence.

As to the defendants in this case, Erskine said, "If you, gentlemen, can think that they were activated by the motive - not of wishing to reform and restore the beautiful fabric of our Constitution, somewhat impaired by time, but to subvert and destroy it ... - an idea at which the mind of every honest man must shudder - you will find them guilty". If that were the result he would give them up even though he was intimately acquainted with them.

But, he continued, it seems the circumstances of the times render any opinion in favour of a reform of Parliament peculiarly improper, and even dangerous ... Were I to address you, gentlemen, to petition for a reform of Parliament, I would address you *now*, because we have seen in other countries the effect of suffering evils to prevail so long in a government, and to increase to such a pitch, that it became impossible to correct them without bringing on greater evils than those which it was the first object of the people to remove; that it became impossible to remedy abuses without opening the door to revolution and anarchy.

The defendants' paper, he said, displayed learning, taste and genius. And God forbid that honest opinion should ever become a crime.

The Judge, Lord Kenyon, summed up to the jury and condescendingly instructed them that the mass of the population could never form a true judgment on political topics. To make sure the jurors appreciated his position and their duty he then added that the paper was published with a wicked malicious intent to vilify the government and make the people discontented with the Constitution under which they lived. On these grounds he considered it to be a gross and seditious libel.

The jury retired for five hours and on their return found the defendants: Guilty of publishing, but with no malicious intent. An angry Lord Kenyon told them, "I cannot record this verdict; it is no verdict at all" and promptly went home to bed. The bewildered jury then withdrew until five o'clock the next morning when they returned with a general verdict of - Not Guilty. The Judge was powerless to do anything but discharge the prisoners.

Rex v. Walker

The next government prosecution of parliamentary reformers took place on April 2, 1794 and was turned by Erskine into something of a farce. Thomas Walker, Samuel Jackson and others from Manchester were charged with conspiring to overthrow the Crown and Constitution; conspiring to aid the French should they succeed in invading the realm; and levying war upon the King.

Six months earlier Walker, a well-known reformer, was subjected to an attack by a "Church and King" crowd who tried to burn down his home and an adjoining warehouse where meetings were sometimes held. Walker, who was a respectable merchant and had been borough-reeve (or Mayor) of Manchester a few years before, had gathered his friends around him and beaten off the mob by firing a volley of cartridges into the air.

It was in this case that the Crown prosecutor Edward Law, later Lord Chief Justice Ellenborough, warned the jury of his opponent. "I know, gentlemen", he said, "what I have most to fear on this occasion; I know the vigour and energy of the mind of my learned friend. I have long felt and admired the powerful effect of his various talents; I know the ingenious sophistry by which he can mislead, and the fascination of that eloquence by which he can subdue the minds of those to whom he addresses himself. I trust it will not be in the power of my friend, by any arts he is able to employ, to seduce you a single step from the sober path of truth and justice".

Erskine was furious but made no response and was able to turn the tables later in the trial when he came to cross-examine the chief witness for the Crown, Thomas Dunn.

As leading counsel for Walker, Erskine soon established that the last of the charges, levying war upon the King, was simply based on Walker having defended his home with the use of guns. The other charges depended chiefly on the evidence of Dunn, a government spy, who after the prosecution was set in train, had gone on his knees to Walker to beg forgiveness for having sworn the charge against him when he was drunk. Asked by Erskine why, now wishing as a Crown witness to retract his apology, he had made it in the first place. Dunn replied, "I went there when I was intoxicated, as I am now". Other witnesses admitted having been instigated to give evidence by a magistrate, the Rev. Mr Griffiths.

Spies, who were often recruited from the Fleet prison, were still a common feature in such trials. Henry Buckle wrote, in his *History of Civilization in England,* "Spies were paid; witnesses were suborned; juries were packed ... The coffee houses, the inns, and the clubs were filled with emissaries of the government, who reported the most hasty expression of common conversation".[6] An example, of course, was furnished in the trial of John Frost.

Some "arms" having been found in Walker's house, Dunn swore that they had been purchased for use in a rebellion which had been planned at meetings he attended. He had seen, he said, men being taught military drill to help French invaders when they came. In cross-examination Erskine demolished his evidence to such effect that the prosecution asked for his arrest on a charge of perjury. For this he was convicted at the same assizes and imprisoned for two years.

Imaginary Armoury

Erskine was also able to prove to the jury that the arms in Walker's house had been purchased solely to defend himself against the attacks of the mob. Such attacks, he smilingly added, being something which the Crown prosecutor, Mr Law, had completely forgotten to mention. The cause of such forgetfulness, Erskine pointed out, was

---

6.   1924.

that the "armoury" would have ill-suited the indictment
or the prosecution evidence. He would, therefore, describe
it himself. This he proceeded to do:

> I was shown last week into this house of conspiracy,
> treason and death, where the arms were kept locked
> up by the prosecution, and saw exposed to view this
> mighty armoury, which was to level the beautiful fabric
> of our Constitution, and to destroy the lives and
> properties of 10 millions of people. It consisted, first,
> of six little swivels, purchased two years ago at the sale
> of Livesay, Hargrave & Co., by Mr Jackson, a
> gentleman of Manchester, who is also one of the
> defendants, and who gave them to Master Walker, a
> boy of about 10 years of age. Swivels, you know, are
> guns so called because they turn upon a pivot; but
> these were taken off their props, were painted and put
> upon blocks resembling carriages of heavy cannon, and
> in that shape may fairly be called "children's toys" ...
> This famous conspiracy had proceeded when they were
> fired on the Prince of Wales's birthday ... I also found
> a little musketoon about so high. I put my thumb upon
> it, when out started a little bayonet, like the jack-in-
> the-box which we buy for children at a fair ... There
> were three or four rusty guns and here or there a
> bayonet or broadsword, covered over with dust and
> rust. These were the arms that had been purchased for
> defence of the day of the riot.

Men had met at Walker's home, Erskine explained,
because they wished the large numbers of people who
were disenfranchised to have a share in the choice of
Members of Parliament. As an example of the necessity
of such reform he mentioned the City of Lancaster. There,
30,000 freeholders returned only two MPs whereas two

boroughs within the county, Clithero and Newton, each contained only a few men who between them could return four Members. Could there be any offence, he asked, in meeting together to consider the wisdom of amending such a system?

Not surprisingly, in the light of all that had been revealed the prosecution case crumbled and the Crown counsel saw the virtue in abandoning it. The jury then returned a verdict of - Not Guilty.

Forensic Faculties

It is no wonder that Lord Brougham who knew Erskine could write, "This consummate advocate appeared to fill at one and the same time different characters; to act as the counsel and representative of the party, and yet to be the very party himself; while he addressed the tribunal, to be also acquainted with every feeling and thought of the Judge or the jury; and while he interrogated the witness whether to draw from him all he knew, and in the most favourable shape, or to shake and displace all he had said that was adverse, he appeared to have entered into the mind of the person he was dealing with, and to be familiar with all that was passing within it".[7]

Indeed, Erskine was virtually always in control of his examination and cross-examination of witnesses. He often persuaded an adverse witness that he was his friend not his enemy and when evidence could not be refuted he would use his charm to reduce its effect. He would not resort to browbeating or rudeness to witnesses, although on one occasion impatience did get the better of him. At

---

7.   Brougham. *Op.cit.* 318.

the trial of Lord Thanet and Cutler Fergusson (of which more later) he was cross-examining Charles Abbott, who afterwards, as Lord Tenterden, became Lord Chief Justice.

After a Bow Street Runner had given evidence, Abbott went into the witness box and gave counsel an evasive answer. "Sir", said Erskine, "I should have been ashamed of the Bow Street Runner if he had given me an answer like that". Abbott's fury was plain to see and he never forgave the retort. Fergusson, who was also a barrister, said this was the only occasion on which he had heard a harsh word from Erskine in conducting a case.

Erskine concentrated his mind on his case and was always able to respond to an emergency. He avoided getting into difficulties himself but would not allow an opposing witness to extricate himself from a dilemma. He never countered a strong argument with a poor one, saying on one occasion, "When a convincing answer cannot be found to an objection, those who understand controversy never give strength to it by a weak one". Above all, perhaps one of his greatest assets in the courtroom was the good humour and bonhomie which radiated from him. As it happens, all these faculties were to the fore in the trial of Thomas Walker.

CHAPTER 9

The State Trials of 1794

Rehearsal in Scotland

In 1792, a number of Scottish reform societies held a Convention in Edinburgh to advocate electoral reform. The very word "Convention" was anathema to the authorities and it came as no shock therefore when some of the delegates were subsequently prosecuted by the government for sedition in recommending the works of Tom Paine. One of them was a young barrister named Thomas Muir who was brought to trial before the High Court of Justiciary in Edinburgh in August 1793.

Lord Braxfield, on whom Robert Louis Stevenson based his *Weir of Hermiston,* was the presiding Judge, and Muir conducted his own defence. Evidence was given that Muir had praised the French financial system and even visited France. This severely displeased the Judge who said, "I never was an admirer of the French but now I can only consider them as monsters in human form". Ironically, Braxfield was himself described by Lord Cockburn, a future Lord Chief Justice of the Queen's Bench, who was present in court as, "a little, dark creature, dressed in black, with silk stockings and white metal buttons, something like one's idea of a puny Frenchman, a most impudent and provoking body".[1]

In his summing up at the end of the trial Lord Braxfield indulged in the following observations:

There were two things, he said, which the jury had to attend to which required no proof. The first was that the British Constitution was the best that ever was since the creation of the world, and it was not possible to make it better. Secondly, there was a spirit of sedition in the country which made every good man uneasy. And the defendant had gone among ignorant country people making them forget their work, and telling them that a reform of the franchise was absolutely necessary for preserving their liberty.

What right, he asked, had they to representation? A government in every country should be just like a corporation, and in Britain it was made up of the landed interest who alone had a right to be represented.

The uncouth Braxfield also whispered to a juror who passed behind the Bench, "come awa', Master Horner, come awa', and help us to hang ane o' thae damned scoundrels". The pliant jury quickly found the prisoner Guilty, whereupon, despite widespread protests, he was sentenced to 14 years' transportation to Botany Bay.

Three other delegates, who had travelled from London, were then tried on similar charges. They challenged the right of Braxfield to sit as their Judge on the clearly justified ground that he was biased against them.

One prisoner, Maurice Margarot, who had been educated at the University of Geneva, even defiantly demanded to examine the Judge from the dock. Braxfield

---

1.   *Examination of the Trials of Sedition ... in Scotland.* ii. 25. 1888.

asked him what questions he wanted to put and the following dialogue ensued:

> Q.   Did you dine at Mr Rochead's at Inverleith in the course of last week?
> A.   And what have you to do with that, Sir?
> Q.   Did any conversation take place with regard to my trial?
> A.   Go on, Sir.
> Q.   Did you use these words: "What should you think of giving him an hundred lashes, together with Botany Bay?" or words to that purpose?
> A.   Go on: put your questions, if you have any more.
> Q.   Did any person, did a lady, say to you that the mob would not allow you to whip me? And, my Lord, did you not say that the mob would be better off for a little blood? These are the questions, my Lord, that I wish to put to you ...

Braxfield.	Do you think I should answer questions of that sort, my Lord Henderland? - (another sitting Judge).
Lord Henderland.	No, my Lord ...
Lord Esgrove.	What may have been said in a private company cannot in any way affect this case ...
Lord Swinton.	My Lord, not one of them are proper.

It occasioned no surprise that Braxfield continued to preside at the trials. Nor, when after another prisoner, Joseph Gerrald, proudly suggested that Jesus Christ was himself a reformer, Braxfield was heard to chuckle from the Bench: "Muckle he made o' that: he was hangit"! Each of the three prisoners was unceremoniously found guilty and duly sentenced to 14 years' transportation.

But these trials and sentences were not merely a Scottish aberration. They had the full support of the government in London where, in the debate on them in the House of Commons, Pitt spoke approvingly of the Judges punishing "such daring delinquents" and suppressing "doctrines so dangerous to the country". Needless to say, this did not prevent a fierce exchange taking place in Parliament to the discredit of Braxfield in the course of which Fox exclaimed, "God help the people who have such Judges". However, the Motion to have the sentences reduced was defeated by the government majority.

As a postscript, the French Government dispatched a warship to intercept and free the transportees, but it failed in its mission. More successfully, sympathisers in the United States, including George Washington and Thomas Jefferson, sent a ship from New York to Botany Bay and Muir was able to escape in it. Although it was later shipwrecked, he managed to survive.

A Panic of Fear

We come now to 1794 and the trial of Thomas Hardy - the shoemaker. There was a great deal of economic distress at the time and this was causing discontent among many sections of the people. But the unrest was in no way out of hand and more menacing were the mindless "Church and King" mobs which were still being activated in support of the government.

The distress did, however, bring into existence a number of Corresponding Societies. Their mere existence in turn inflamed unnecessary fear in the hearts of an already rash government. The most influential of them were the Constitutional Society, the Society for Constitutional Information and the London Corresponding Society. That their members were drawn from different circles of society is revealed by their subscription rates. Five guineas a year was the cost of joining the first; two and a half guineas to gain admission to the second and one penny a week for the last. Between them they undoubtedly enjoyed widespread support.

In a panic fuelled by such fear, in May 1794, the government, as a first step, arrested 12 members of these Societies including John Horne Tooke, a philologist who was a leading light in the first two, Thomas Hardy, who was Secretary of the London Corresponding Society and John Thelwall, an avowed Jacobin. At the same time they suspended Habeas Corpus and announced the discovery of a huge revolutionary plot.

As Macaulay perceptively saw it: "In Pitt's domestic policy there was at this time assuredly no want of vigour. While he offered to French Jacobins a resistance so feeble that it only encouraged the evil which he wished to suppress, he put down English Jacobinism with a strong hand ... It was hardly safe for a republican to avow his political creed over his beefsteak and his bottle of port at a chophouse ... He [Pitt] was all feebleness and languor in his conflict with the foreign enemy who was really to be dreaded, and reserved all his energy and resolution for the domestic enemy who might safely have been despised".[2]

For six months the prisoners were incarcerated in the Tower of London. From there they were frequently taken

---

2.   *A History of England in the Eighteenth Century.* Folio Society edn. 1988/9. 1980.

to the Privy Council for interrogation. Sorrow, as well as ill-health brought on by their surroundings, depressed them. Particularly in Hardy's case when his wife suffered an attack on their house by a "Church and King" mob and died in childbirth, leaving an unfinished note to her despairing husband saying, "You are never out of my thoughts, sleeping or waking".

As part of the psychological warfare against Hardy and the others, Pitt, who was personally involved in the preparations for the trial, took to the House of Commons three huge sealed bags of captured documents and a message from the King requiring the enactment of a Special Powers Act. That their lives were at risk was re-enforced when Edmund Burke accused them of being assassins and urged that the disease of the body politic demanded the "critical terrors of the cautery and the knife".[3]

Yet the accused had merely called a Convention (that word again!) to seek means of securing reform in the representation of the people in Parliament. They had said nothing against the King and by no means were they all republicans or Jacobins. Indeed in 1793 one branch of the London Corresponding Society had actually called for the expulsion of members advocating levelling principles. Notwithstanding their acknowledged moderation, the prisoners were charged with high treason in "compassing the death of the King" although it was never suggested that they actually threatened the life of the King or intended to any use force whatsoever.

Pitt wanted a repeat of the intimidating Scottish scenario but failed to take into account Erskine, the widespread support for Fox and the Whigs who opposed

---

3.   Thomas Hardy. *Memoir.* 42/3. 1832.

coercion and the more independent spirit of the ordinary
English jury.

Trial of the Shoemaker

Erskine was assigned to all the prisoners at their request
and, as was usual in treason trials, he conducted these
epoch-making defences without fee. On the accused
declining to be tried jointly, the Attorney-General, Sir
John Scott (an ally of Pitt and afterwards the dilatory
Lord Chancellor Eldon) selected Thomas Hardy to be
dealt with first. This was the prisoner against whom he
mistakenly thought he could make the strongest case. In
fact, Thelwall would probably have been a better choice.
As usual, Erskine prepared his case with care and
confidence.

The trial commenced at the Old Bailey on October 28,
before Lord Chief Justice Eyre and several other Judges.[4]
Erskine's junior was Vicary Gibbs, little known at the
time but from this case to go on to become Attorney-
General and Chief Justice of the Common Pleas. Despite
being a Tory and a government supporter he played a
robust part in the defence.

Opening the case against Hardy, Sir John Scott
produced an enormous mass of documents which covered
the whole table of the court and he spoke for nine hours.
It is noteworthy that until this time there had never been
a trial for high treason that had lasted longer than a day.
This was to continue for eight days.

When midnight approached on the first day Erskine
suggested an adjournment in order that the jurors might

---

4.   24 *State Trials*. 199. 1818.

be permitted to go home for the night. This was objected to by the prosecution as unprecedented but the Court decided to rise and the jurors were locked up in a tavern near the courthouse. It was also arranged that the court would sit each day from 8 am to the early hours after midnight. However, before the jury were escorted to their billet, Erskine gave them something to think about other than Scott's lengthy opening speech by asking, in their presence, to be allowed to examine the mass of papers in court *which he indicated the prosecution and the Privy Council had refused to let him see.*

The case for the prosecution, but not the evidence, was that the prisoner was sympathetic to the French Republic, with whom Britain was then at war, and wanted a similar revolution in England to that which had taken place in France. Erskine tackled the defence courageously and himself spoke to the jury for seven hours. As with all Erskine's speeches, it is impossible to convey its full flavour by limited extracts but Horne Tooke wrote of it that, "This speech will live for ever".[5]

Referring to the alleged possibility of meetings leading to disorder, Erskine took his usual position and said, "I protest in his [Hardy's] name against all speculations respecting *consequences* when the law commands us to look only to *intentions*".

As far as "compassing the King's death" was concerned, he outlined the law of treason and said that in this case it was quite impossible to understand the evidence against Hardy who could not possibly be proved to be guilty of intending to destroy the King, as the law required.

He proceeded to show that the London Corresponding

---

5.   *Ibid.* 877.

Society had, in fact, only adopted the doctrines of Pitt the Elder, and that the Duke of Richmond had gone much further than Hardy. He had indeed in some respects particularly in advocating universal suffrage and annual parliaments. However, Erskine produced him and Richard Brinsley Sheridan as witnesses for the defence. They both gave evidence that they supported the aims of the Convention and knew well that Hardy was a law-abiding citizen.

Pointing out that Prime Minister Pitt had once been a reformer, not only like his father before him but also like Hardy, Erskine claimed that, "It would be the height of injustice and wickedness to torture expressions, and pervert conduct into treason and rebellion which had recently lifted others up to love of the nation, to the confidence of the Sovereign and to all the honours of the State".

As *The Edinburgh Review* was to see it, Pitt had "committed in his youth the sin of reform; - now he had his atonement to make for an offence only pardonable on the score of that heedless and tender age - only to be expiated by the most glaring proofs of amendment". To this end, the journal claimed, he had turned to corruption and power.[6]

It was claimed that this article was written by Henry Brougham. Indeed, Pitt's close friend, Lord Melville, regarded it as so disrespectful of Pitt that he wanted Brougham put out of Parliament, although how this could be effected he did not say. Hearing of the proposal Brougham wrote in a letter to his friend Thomas Creevey that without admitting he had written the article he was

---

6.   *Op.cit.* 120.

ready to avow all it contained.[7]

Erskine continued by asserting that more than 40,000 people had corresponded with the Constitutional Information Society and other societies, and would now face a campaign of terror worse than that of Judge Jeffreys if the liberty of the prisoner were destroyed.

As to the alleged sympathy of the Societies with the French Republic, Erskine carefully drew the jury into considering the effects of the continental powers' efforts to extinguish liberty in France by force of arms. He then went on to say:

Men may assert the right of every people to choose their government without seeking to destroy their own. This accounts for many expressions imputed to the unfortunate prisoners, which I have often uttered myself, and shall continue to utter every day of my life, and call upon the spies of government to record them. I will say anywhere without fear - nay, I will say in this court where I stand, - that "an attempt to interfere by despotic combination and violence with any government which a people choose to give to themselves, whether it be good or evil, is an oppression and subversion of the natural and inalienable rights of man"; and, though the government of this country should countenance such a system, it would not only be still legal for me to express my detestation of it, as I here deliberately express it, but it would become my interest and my duty to do so.

---

7.   Letter in 1810. *The Creevey Papers*. Folio Society edn. 1970. When Brougham became Lord Chancellor as Baron Brougham and Vaux, Creevey mischievously nicknamed him "Guy Vaux".

Spies and Informers

Commenting to the jury on the evidence of a prosecution witness and government spy called Grove, Erskine said that the witness had professed to speak from notes but had frequently looked up to the ceiling when giving evidence. Further, Erskine reminded them, when he had asked him at one point if he was then speaking from a note Grove had answered that what he was saying was from recollection. "Good God Almighty!", thundered Erskine to the jury: "Recollection mixing itself up with notes in a case of *high treason* ... Oh, excellent evidence!".

A similar incident occurred when another witness with notes, on being asked for the date of a meeting replied that he thought it was *about* a particular date. "None of your thinking when you have the paper in your hand", exclaimed Erskine. "What date have you taken, good Mr Spy?"

Witness.	I do not think on such an occasion being a spy is any disgrace.
Chief Justice Eyre.	(to Erskine) These observations are more proper when you come to address the jury.
Attorney-General.	Really that is not a proper way to examine witnesses. Lord Holt held strong language to such sort of an address from a counsel to a witness who avowed himself a spy.
Erskine.	I am sure I shall always pay that attention to the court which is due from me but I am

	not to be told by the Attorney-General how I am to examine a witness!
Attorney-General.	I thought you had not heard his Lordship.
Erskine.	I am much obliged to his Lordship for the admonition he gave me. I heard his Lordship, and I heard you - whom I should not have heard.

Yet another witness, Henry Alexander, was also a government spy and informer. On his testimony also the life of Hardy was at risk. Erskine set out to demolish his evidence and at one point when questioning him mercilessly the Judge intervened to tell Erskine to "give him fair play". Erskine was astonished. "He has certainly had fair play", he retorted, "I wish we had as fair play - but that is not intended to the court".

The celebrated counsel William Garrow, as one of the prosecutors, immediately rose and asked whom Erskine had meant if not the court. Erskine merely replied that the prisoner had a right to fair play. Garrow persisted and when Erskine refused to enter into an altercation Garrow repeated his question. Erskine then replied that he would not be called to order by the Bar and returned to the witness.

Acquittal

By the end of his speech, which lasted from 2 pm to 9 pm, Erskine was so exhausted and hoarse that he could only whisper his peroration to the jury and express confidence that they would ensure that justice prevailed. Despite his affliction his quietly-spoken words swept around the still courtroom and, when he finished, there was uproar in his favour which spread to the people still crowding the streets around the court. He then went outside and managed to speak to the crowds, urging them to await the verdict with confidence in the law and to do nothing that would endanger the lives of the accused.

Despite all the preparation and pressure of the government the jury found Hardy Not Guilty, to the rapturous rejoicing of the multitude. The tension of the trial so affected the foreman of the jury, a Mr Buck of Acton, that on the jury's return to the court he delivered the verdict in a whisper and then fainted on the spot.

After the trial the Solicitor-General expressed chagrin and surprise at the acquittal, as did the government. In contrast, however, Henry Addington, at the time Speaker of the House of Commons, commented that, although counsel for the Crown were too lax in defining treason, he saw little cause for surprise and uneasiness at the verdict.

Almost alone in the country he thought the jury were wholly uninfluenced by Erskine's "strange doctrines upon the law of treason" and that the case had been made out, despite the verdict. Nevertheless, he concluded, it was more important to maintain the credit of a mild and unprejudiced administration of justice than even to convict a Jacobin.[8] On all counts he seems to have been curiously out of touch with what had been going on.

On the other hand, to the satisfaction of the *Edinburgh Review* Erskine had proved how much a single man could do against the corruption of his age and how far he could

---

8.		George Pellew. *Life of Viscount Sidmouth.* i. 132. 1847.

vindicate the liberties of his country.[9]

Erskine's own thoughts at the time are revealed in a letter he wrote to his friend Dr Samuel Parr,

> I have a thousand thanks to send you for your kind and friendly letter. The approbation of such an excellent judge of every accomplishment is a great prize; and I hope to be a candidate for it to better effect in a few months, when Gurney [the shorthand writer in court] publishes the proceedings, of which you have as yet but an imperfect sketch. Let me also thank Mrs Parr for her partial judgment, and I hope that in a few months she will be a complete convert to reform of Parliament ...
>
> P.S. Our friend Sheridan has been a constant attendant on the trial, and gave most important evidence for Hardy.

John Horne Tooke

To widespread amazement after the acquittal of Hardy, the government persisted in the charge of high treason against his co-accused, John Horne Tooke. The case is of interest in itself but, because of Tooke's irreverence towards the court, it also reveals something of the mode of criminal trials in the reign of George III.

Apart from the speech of Erskine, there is the scrupulously fair conduct of Lord Chief Justice Eyre - a style unknown in almost all earlier State Trials and in sharp contrast to the conduct of Lord Braxfield. And, perhaps most remarkable to lawyers today, the constant

---

9. *Op.cit.* 127.

interventions by the prisoner with his frequent arguments, interruptions, and questions to the witnesses and the Lord Chief Justice himself. At that time in all criminal trials, not merely for treason, a courtroom often resembled a bear-garden with the Judge, the jury, the lawyers and the witnesses all joining in when the mood took them.

The trial of Tooke, who was nearly 60 years old, commenced on November 17, with huge friendly crowds again surging around the Old Bailey and its precincts.

A respected philologist and a wit, Tooke had earlier been elected to Parliament for the notorious rotten borough of Old Sarum, a constituency in which the electors were the landowner, "an old woman, and a pig". The return was successfully challenged on the ground that as a former clergyman he was ineligible for election and the House of Commons debarred him. He failed to become a barrister on a similar ruling, with perhaps some loss to the English Bar.

At one time Tooke defended himself in an action brought against him by Charles James Fox for the expenses of yet another Westminster election petition. He began his address to the jury in this case: "Gentlemen, there are here three parties to be considered - you, Mr Fox and myself. As for the Judge and the crier, they are sent here to preserve order, and they are both well paid for their trouble".

When the trial for treason opened, Tooke was asked, in the normal manner, how he would be tried. He replied, whilst emphatically shaking his head, "I would be tried by God and my country" (ie, by a jury) "But ..." here he paused as if he feared the Judges would be swayed by the solemn pledge the government had made that he would be punished. Indeed, in prison he had prepared a speech to be made to the court in which he proposed to argue violently about that pledge in detail, but the earlier acquittal of Hardy had made him more sanguine as to his own fate and it remained undelivered.

Nevertheless, the government persisted in its determination and its biased approach. As we have seen, Pitt had judged the case important enough to take a personal part in preparing it. And when, in examination by the Privy Council prior to the trial, a prosecution witness, William Sharpe, refused to be intimidated, Pitt said in front of him in the manner of Lord Braxfield and with a gesture of despair, "Well! We can do without his evidence. Let him be sent to prison and hanged with the rest of them in the Tower".

Soon after the trial had commenced Horne Tooke asked to be able to sit with his counsel. Lord Eyre responded that this was an indulgence very rarely granted to a prisoner. Tooke replied that his Lordship would forgive him but he claimed it as his right by law and not as an indulgence. He then added, "My Lord, you have no indulgence to show; you are bound to be just". His life and the well-being of his family, he said, were at stake and as he had been denied any knowledge of the case against him he needed to sit with his counsel in order to provide a full defence.

The Judges acceded to the request but only on the ground that it was desirable since the prisoner's health had deteriorated gravely whilst he was held in the Tower. They also ruled that although the law was clear that the court should not rise during the trial, in view of its likely length they would sit from 9 am to 9 pm each day.

Once seated at the table with his counsel Tooke showed, in the words of Lord John Campbell, that he was: "Cool and prompt, ready at repartee and fond of notoriety, he trod the boards of the Old Bailey like some amateur actor pleased with his part, and resolved to make the most of it, even though the catastrophe should terminate in his death".[10]

In fact, Tooke's interventions in the proceedings, including the cross-examinations of witnesses, were as frequent as those of his counsel, who took them all in good humour. And at times when he argued questions of evidence wrongly, he would take a pinch of snuff and quietly apologize by saying that he was only a student of 40 years standing!

However, on one occasion he objected to the admissibility of evidence of a particular fact on the ground that he was not connected with it. Eyre reminded him that if there were two or three links to make a chain, they must go to one first, and then to another, and see whether the chain was made.

Horne Tooke	(in reply). I beg your pardon, my Lord, but is not a chain composed of links? and may I not disjoin each link? and do I not thereby destroy the chain?
Eyre, CJ.	I rather think not until the links are put together, and form the chain.
Horne Tooke.	Nay, my Lord, with great submission to your Lordship, I rather think that I may, because it is my business to prevent the forming of that chain.

Among the witnesses called by Erskine to support Tooke's call for reform and testify to their knowledge of Tooke and his learned pursuits were again the Duke of Richmond and Richard Brinsley Sheridan, both of whom it will be recalled had given evidence for Hardy. In addition, there

---

10.   *Op.cit.* 486.

were the Bishop of Gloucester, Earl Stanhope, Earl Camden and Charles James Fox.

Horne Tooke had in the past turned the tables on many a Judge and advocate and now he enjoyed the irony and pleasure of issuing a subpoena to William Pitt requiring him also to give evidence. The Prime Minister was forced, reluctantly, after the evidence given by Sheridan, to remember that he had himself at one time attended meetings composed of delegates to recommend parliamentary reform. And, of course, earlier we have noted his letters to the attorney, John Frost.

This admission virtually destroyed the prosecution case that delegate meetings to advocate reform were merely a device to cloak the organizing of treasonable insurrection. The prosecutor continued undeterred however, and produced amongst others the witness William Sharpe, an engraver, who had to give formal evidence of Horne Tooke's presence at a meeting of the legal Constitutional Information Society, as if that were itself treason. In addition, they called a government informer who had been sent to spy on Tooke in his home and had been led along by Tooke into believing that a national insurrection was imminent. His report, which was based solely on Tooke's fictions, was not surprisingly laughed out of court.

Ridicule

The case against Tooke rested chiefly on a letter sent to him by another prisoner, Jeremiah Joyce, which the prosecution had intercepted and Tooke never received. This short letter gave the news of the arrest of Hardy and concluded with the sentence: "Query: is it possible to get ready by Thursday?" In Parliament, in endeavouring to inflame public feeling against the prisoner, the government had interpreted this sentence as indicating preparation for insurrection which might be got "ready by Thursday".

Sharpe testified that all Tooke had undertaken was to collect from the Court Calendar a list of titles, offices and pensions bestowed by Pitt upon himself, his relations, friends and dependants. Anxious to receive the list Joyce had asked if it could be ready by Thursday. To make matters more ridiculous the government had sent a troop of Light Dragoons on a futile foray to the neighbourhood of Tooke's home at Wimbledon to look out for whatever was to be ready by Thursday. Nothing incriminating was found.

In his address to the jury, Erskine poured scorn on the government's attempts to link Tooke with an armed rebellion. The prisoner, he declared, was a gentleman who rarely left his home. And even the solitary pike which had "formerly glared rebellion" in the court had been taken away. There was, he said, nothing in *The Arabian Nights* or *The Tales of the Fairies* to compare with the prosecution fantasies. The speech as a whole combined powerful reasoning, eloquence and tact and caused intense applause in the courtroom.

In sharp contrast was the conduct of Sir John Scott, the Attorney-General. After complaining of some remarks made about how he had come to institute the prosecutions he said he could endure anything but an attack on his good name which was the "little patrimony" he could leave to his children. Upon that he burst into tears, which for him was not unusual. The Solicitor-General, Sir John Mitford, then began to sob in sympathy with him, which was unusual.

Tooke, fearing the effect of these melodramatics upon the jury, exclaimed in a loud whisper, "Do you know what

Sir John Mitford is crying about? He is thinking of the destitute condition of Sir John Scott's children, and the little patrimony they are likely to divide among them".

After the Judge had summed up it took the jury only eight minutes without leaving the box to return a verdict of Not Guilty which, as with Hardy, caused rejoicing among the crowds outside the court. Erskine's horses were taken from his carriage amidst bonfires and blazing tableaux and he was drawn by the crowds to his home in the Temple. Here, from a window he declared that injured innocence still obtained protection from a British jury and then asked the people to disperse peacefully.

Victory

Despite the acquittals of Hardy and Horne Tooke the Crown blindly continued with the prosecution of a third prisoner. This was John Thelwall, a lecturer who, spies alleged, had cut the froth from a pint of porter and advocated the same fate for the heads of kings. Notwithstanding this terrible treason, the Lord Chief Justice felt it safe, after the acquittals in the earlier cases, to sleep throughout the Attorney-General's speech on this occasion!

Thelwall, who undoubtedly had a well-endowed intellect and was a true Jacobin, was full of self-conceit and tried to emulate Horne Tooke by intervening in the proceedings. But, aware of the difference between the two men, this time Erskine would have none of it.

In desperation the accused then wrote a note to his counsel saying, "I will plead my own case". Erskine tersely replied, "If you do you will be hanged". Thelwall, considering discretion to be the better part of valour, thereupon returned, "Then I will be hanged if I do". He too was found not guilty and the government finally had to scrap 800 warrants of arrest which had been prepared for immediate use following the anticipated convictions.

Erskine, and the juries who came under his spell, thus prevented the government from using the doctrine of constructive treason to fetter freedom of speech as well as earlier preventing the law of libel from being used to the same end. Lord Brougham was to say that if the people still enjoyed the possibility of free discussion about their rulers and their Constitution without dying the death of a traitor it was due to this great man.

Writing on the trials of Hardy and Tooke as he was, Brougham concluded that Erskine's "dauntless energy, his indomitable courage, kindling his eloquence, inspiring his conduct, giving direction and lending firmness to his matchless skill, resisted the combination of statesmen, and princes, and lawyers - the league of cruelty and craft, formed to destroy our liberties - and triumphantly scattered to the winds the half-accomplished scheme of an unsparing proscription. Before such a precious service as this may the lustre of statesmen and orators grow pale".[11] It was a fitting, and generous, tribute from one famous lawyer to another.

From this time on Erskine enjoyed undisputed ascendancy in the courts and was regarded as the advocate of freedom and liberty of speech in state trials.

---

11.   *Historical Sketches. Op.cit.*

CHAPTER 10

Tyranny, War, Riot and Blasphemy

"I Will Never Die a Slave"

On January 5, 1795, Erskine received an unusually friendly reception in the House of Commons when he spoke in support of Sheridan's Motion for the repeal of the Act by which Habeas Corpus had been suspended. He took the opportunity to censure the government for the recent State Trials and said the juries in the trials of Hardy and the others had revealed the falsehood and absurdity of the alleged sedition and conspiracy. He went on to ask who would defend the country if the threat of invasion from France came about. Only the people could do it and they would only if they felt they were defending liberty.[1]

Later in the year, on November 17, he made a strong speech against the Seditious Meeting Bill, the first of the notorious "Two Acts", which made most public meetings illegal. Erskine exclaimed that he would repeat again and

---

1.   31 *Parliamentary History*. 1087. 1795.

again that, as the justly honoured Pitt the Elder, (the "Great Commoner") had said, it was the right of a people to resist a government which exercised tyranny. If necessary, they should not surrender their birthright to a despotic Minister but should defend their freedom by the last extremity to which free men could resort.

"For my part", Erskine concluded, "I shall never cease to struggle in support of liberty. In no situation will I desert the cause. I was born a free man, and, by God, I will never die a slave".[2]

Busy now in Parliament, at the end of that same month Erskine delivered a fine, impassioned speech against the Treasonable Activities Bill which became the second of the "Two Acts". This amended the law of treason so that an overt act would no longer be required to prove a "conspiracy to levy war". Speaking or writing would be sufficient. Once again he made a masterly exposition of the Statute of Treason of 1352, the tyrannical constructions added to it by the courts, and now the Bill whereby "a sigh or a groan" might be construed as treason. A false alarm had been sounded throughout the kingdom, he said, and was echoed back by spies and informers.

In the trials of Hardy and Horne Tooke, Chief Justice Eyre had held that a presumption of law was sufficient to find the prisoners guilty of treason but the jury refused to accept his direction to that effect. No doubt, the new statute was intended to avert that possibility arising again. Curiously, Lord Ellenborough thought it unnecessary because, he said, the jury in the State Trials were perverse. How such perversity should be overcome he did not say.

---

2.   32 *Ibid.* 310.

However, subsequently, in *Rex v. Watson* in 1817 he had come to accept that the statute was helpful in that it, "... did not so much introduce any new treasons, as declare to be substantive treasons those acts which had been, by successive constructions of the Statute of Treason, determined to be the strongest and more pregnant overt acts of the several treasons specified in that statute".[3] But, apart from the perils posed by constructive treasons, he was overlooking some aspects of the new Act which were precisely what made it even more obnoxious.

The original statute was sufficient to protect the King and his government, explained Erskine. The new Bill wantonly created new and undefined treasons which would disorganize the country's jurisprudence and by sanctioning grievous and vexatious measures, only excite disaffection and discord.[4]

Society Against Republicans

At the same time as he was vigorously attacking the "Two Acts", Erskine and his Whig friends took a surprising step which violated their normal precept of free discussion. John Reeves, a writer of some distinction, published a book entitled *Thoughts on the English Government* in which he argued that the monarchy could function without Parliament as it had done in the past. It was a mild essay by the president of the "Society against Republicans and Levellers".

The defender of Thomas Hardy and many others now

---

3.   32 *State Trials*. 579.
4.   32 *Parl. Hist.* 470. 1795.

supported a resolution that the book was a breach of the privileges of the House of Commons and that the author should be prosecuted for libel. Otherwise, said Erskine in explanation, and with some logic, the public would see them as being in favour of the Crown against the rights of the people. Reeves was brought for trial before Lord Kenyon on May 20, 1796, when the jury, believing the book was an improper publication, nevertheless did not question the honesty of his motives and in line with Erskine's reasoning in earlier trials found him, Not Guilty.

Prosecuting the War

After negotiations for peace with the French Republic failed in 1796, Pitt moved an address in the House calling for a more vigorous prosecution of the war. It was to Erskine that fell the task of speaking to an opposition amendment. Observing that "France had formerly offered terms, the obtaining of which now would make the right honourable gentleman be worshipped as a god", Erskine suddenly lost control of what he was saying, and abruptly sat down. Later, Creevey was to write that, Pitt's speech was "all for war and war without end". But he also observed that Erskine "followed [Pitt] in the most confused, unintelligible, inefficient performance that ever came from the mouth of man".[5]

Undoubtedly Erskine was feeling unwell from the effects of overwork in his practice at the Bar. And, although Fox promptly and successfully took over his mantle in urging peace, for several years thereafter

---

5.   *The Creevey Papers. Op.cit.* 15/16.

Erskine rarely attended the debates of the House or spoke there.

During this period, however, he published a pamphlet entitled, *A View of the Causes and Consequences of the Present War with France* which ran into an amazing 37 editions. Its themes were that Britain had completely abandoned the principles which the allies claimed were the justification of hostilities, and that peace should be now sought as it should have been in 1792 when France was eager to negotiate.

When his close friend, Dr Samuel Parr, known as the "Whig Johnson" congratulated him on the work, Erskine modestly for once, wrote in reply, "I wonder it is not nonsense from beginning to end, for I wrote it amidst constant interruption, a great part of it in open court during the trial of causes".

In the pamphlet Erskine could not avoid referring again to the need for parliamentary reform in order to preserve the Constitution and avert republicanism, or Pitt's change of attitude towards it. He pointed out that Pitt the Elder had recognized that the corrupt condition of Parliament had caused the breach with the American colonists, and that his son had accepted his legacy and at first attempted to remedy the corruption, before turning his back on reform in order to protect his position as Minister. This angered Pitt who referred to the pamphlet with bitter scorn.

The main thrust of the pamphlet, however, was a call for peace with France linked with a demand for a real improvement in the economic conditions of the people and steps to make justice available to the poor. But the pamphlet had to contend with the pro-war outpourings of Burke whose spurious patriotism and mania about France were sweeping the nation. In consequence, there was a horror of everything connected with France, even

liberty because the French claimed to be contending for
it.

In this connexion Erskine wrote, "The writings of Mr
Burke have had a great and extensive influence in
producing and continuing this fatal contest" (ie, the war).
"Let us avail ourselves, then, of the great wisdom of his
former writings" (against the war with the American
colonists) "to lay the foundations of peace".

In this chilling atmosphere William Stone, a London
merchant, was charged with high treason in allegedly
conspiring to invite an invasion from France. On his
behalf in court, Erskine dealt with the evidence in
masterly fashion to show that Stone was not guilty. It
was not enough, he then observed to the jury, for the
Crown to raise so thick a cloud that they could not be
sure which way to walk. A clear light had to be shed upon
the path leading to conviction, before they could venture
to tread it. During a long retirement the jury seemed
unable to find any such illumination and returning to
court pronounced the prisoner, Not Guilty.

Clerical Riot

At Shrewsbury in July 1796 the Bishop of Bangor and
others were prosecuted for riot and asked Erskine to
defend them. The Bishop and some of his clergy had
broken into the office of the registrar of the Consistorial
Court of Bangor and ejected a Mr Grindley who they said
was falsely claiming to be the lawful registrar. Grindley
indicted them all for riot and assault.

Erskine was duly briefed for the defendants who clearly
had acted unlawfully, although they tried to make light
of it as a mere prank. In his opening speech the
prosecution counsel, William Adam, referred to Erskine's

earlier defence of another church dignitary, the Dean of St Asaph, in the same court on a similar charge. "They who heard my Learned Friend upon that occasion", he said, "they who have read the history of that period, cannot forget the uninterrupted stream of splendid eloquence and of powerful ability, which has been rolling on, with increasing force, from that period to the present moment".

In opening his own speech to the jury Erskine referred to the kindness of his opponent's remarks but said that despite it all he did not know how best to address them. It was difficult not to confuse the mildness of manner of prosecuting counsel with that of his client who in reality had set on foot a prosecution hatched in mischief and in malice.

In this case Erskine decided not to risk calling any evidence and provoking cross-examination, and made a virtue of the fact in what was a rather tortuous speech to the jury. Mr Justice Heath, who was not inclined towards Erskine and sometimes said, "I am always on my guard against these 300 guinea gentry", summed up for a conviction. However, the jury acquitted the Bishop and his clergy, perhaps because of their ages and calling.

As far as fees are concerned, by this time Erskine was said to be earning £10,000 a year; by "active employment" he had written to his brother, the Earl of Buchan, on Christmas Day, 1791. This was £1,600 more than any other counsel had ever made. On the other hand, despite his great success at the Bar, his liberal opinions and consistent support of Fox, whom the King and Pitt still hated, ensured that he received no official appointment whilst Pitt was Prime Minister.

That this rankled is clear from a letter he wrote when, after Pitt had retired in 1801, Addington offered him the post of Attorney-General. The letter dated December 28, was written to Nathaniel Bond, one of the Lords of the Treasury. Erskine wrote, "I consider that Mr Addington felt, as he ought to do, the very high station I have maintained for four-and-twenty years in the profession; and that he further felt a satisfaction, from private regard, in expressing the pleasure it would give him to see me serving the public on stations which my birth and acquired place rendered fit for me".[6]

As we shall see, failing to obtain the support of the Prince of Wales, Erskine declined the offer. It is difficult to see why Erskine thought this a sufficient reason to reject such an opportunity, particularly as the Prince offered no objection but merely made no comment. However, that, no doubt, was enough to signify his displeasure of the proposal and as Erskine's patron and friend that was enough.

"Age of Reason"

We now approach a most unexpected scene - Erskine prosecuting for blasphemous libel. And, Part II of Tom Paine's *The Age of Reason* for good measure. On this occasion, in 1797, the government declined to prosecute in order not to cause a vast increase in the sales of the book as had happened with Part II of *The Rights of Man*.

However, the Society for the Suppression of Vice and Immorality considered the book to be a profane attack on the Christian religion and, with Paine still in France,[7] indicted a bookseller named Thomas Williams at whose

---

6.   George Pellew. *Op.cit.* i. 477.
7.   Paine had quarrelled with Robespierre and was being held in appalling conditions in a Paris dungeon whilst awaiting the guillotine. He was later freed when Robespierre fell.

shop it had been sold. They also decided to instruct Erskine as prosecuting counsel. Having defended Paine and his *Rights of Man* it is curious to see Erskine now prosecuting Paine's new book.

James Ridgway, the editor who published many of Erskine's speeches, considered that his address to the jury in this case revealed that the stand he took in the *Rights of Man* case was merely that of an advocate and did not represent his own views. This cannot be sustained, however, when one reads Erskine's sentiments on liberty and a free press in his speech in defence of Tom Paine. To some extent they were subsumed in the present case by Erskine's deeply held biblical beliefs which Paine was endeavouring to expose.

Paine had imbued the principles of the Quakers and Methodists and was a believer in God and natural religion. He considered Christianity contained good moral precepts but also had a bloody history of bigotry with its crusade against Islam, its persecution of Jews and its enslavement of Africans. On the other hand, Erskine was a devoted Christian and may well have considered Paine's submitting the established religion to scrutiny and ridicule to be truly blasphemous. Nonetheless, to prosecute a man for selling *The Age of Reason* was contrary to all his previous principles, and he lived to regret it.

Erskine told the jury that he was deeply devoted to the truths of Christianity, not only from the teachings of his parents but also from the reflections and understanding of his riper years. Against Paine's suggestion that Christianity was but a fable, Erskine invoked the names of Newton, Boyle, Locke and Milton to argue the contrary. Whether he personally needed such corroboration is doubtful because he also said he had no fear of the reasoning of Deists like Paine since Christ had said, "if it be of God, it will stand".

On the principle of free speech, which he always believed had improved governments and religions, Erskine agreed that every man had the right to investigate, with decency, controversial points of the Christian religion. But no man, consistently with a law which only existed under its sanctions, had a right to deny its very existence. The importance of honest motive in cases of libel which he had raised so often in the past was overlooked.

What concerned him now was that he believed the book was mischievous in its effects. It struck at the best, and sometimes the only, refuge and consolation amidst the distress and afflictions of the world. "The poor and humble", he said, "whom it affects to pity, may be stabbed to the heart by it. They have more occasion for firm hopes beyond the grave than the rich and prosperous, who have other comforts to render life delightful".

Erskine's Mantle

Ironically, counsel for the defence was none other than Stewart Kyd who had been a co-defendant with Hardy and Horne Tooke in the earlier treason trials in which Erskine had so ably succeeded. Kyd, in fact, adopted many of the arguments that Erskine had previously used in criminal libel trials. For instance, he claimed that the whole book should be considered and not merely the passages which were read out by the prosecutor.

The real question, Kyd told the jury, was not whether they or the Judge approved the book, or shared the author's opinion. It was whether the author believed in what he wrote and meant seriously to examine an important subject without a malevolent intention to do mischief. However, when Kyd began to deal with some of the stories in the Bible which Paine had described as immoral the Judge, Lord Kenyon, interrupted to say that he could not sit in court and hear that kind of discussion.

All eyes must have turned to Erskine when Kyd donned his mantle and replied to the Judge, "My Lord, I stand here on the privilege of an advocate in an English court of justice. This man has applied to me to defend him. I have undertaken his defence; and I have often heard your Lordship declare that every man has a right to be defended. I know no other mode by which I can seriously defend him against this charge, than the way which I am now pursuing. If your Lordship wishes to prevent me from pursuing it, you may as well tell me to abandon my duty to my client at once". No doubt taken aback at this display, Lord Kenyon merely replied, "Go on Sir".

Kyd then continued that if the Christian religion was founded in truth the more it was examined the more it would be firmly established in the minds of men. To punish for disputing its truth was to admit it would not bear the test of a rigid scrutiny.

As prosecutor, Erskine was in the unusual position for him of having the last word as counsel. He accepted the sincerity of Kyd but thought that public renunciation of the truths of religion upon which the government and the Constitution rested must be a serious crime.

In summing up the Judge called the book a nefarious publication with malignant purposes and the Special Jury needed no time to find the bookseller, Guilty.

Paine wrote to Erskine to deplore the very existence of Special Juries nominated by the Crown. They were comprised, he said, of London merchants who if spoken to about scripture would understand it to mean scrip and tell how much it was worth at the Stock Exchange. As for

theology they would say that they knew no such
gentleman on the Exchange. "Tell them", he said, "it is
in the Bible and they will lay a bowl of punch it is not,
and leave it to the parson of the parish to decide".

Christian Charity

As was not unusual at the time, Williams was allowed to
be at liberty for seven months before being brought back
to court for sentence. During this period Erskine
happened to pass one day through the narrow Old
Turnstile passage in Holborn on the way to his house in
Lincoln's Inn Fields when a woman in his path tugged at
his coat. Emaciated with disease and sorrow she was
bathed in tears. She managed to pull him to a small hovel
in the passage where he found the bookseller Williams,
whom he had helped to convict, sitting with his three
children all suffering from smallpox.

The poor man was busy sewing up religious tracts,
which apparently had always been his principal
employment. Seeing Erskine he promised to find copies
of *The Age of Reason* still in circulation and bring them
in to be destroyed. Erskine was to write later that the
scene affected him most deeply and that he was fully
convinced that Williams's poverty and not his will had led
him to sell the book.

At this time he concluded that what he had witnessed
would afford a happy opportunity for the prosecutors to
vindicate and render universally popular the cause in
which they had succeeded. In other words to show true
Christian charity rather than ruin a helpless family to
whom they could show mercy.

Accordingly, he recommended this course to the
Society. However, at a meeting with the Bishops of

London, Durham and St Asaph present the Society decided that it could not bring itself to exercise lenity. On receiving the news of this Erskine immediately refused to continue to represent such "hard hearted" Christians further and returned his retainer. He wrote later that, "Such a voluntary society, however respectable or useful, having received no injury could not erect itself into a *custos morum* and claim a right to dictate to counsel, who had consented to be employed on the part of the King for the ends of justice only".[8]

When Williams finally stood before Mr Justice Ashurst for sentence the Judge said the court would not pass so severe a sentence as perhaps it should only on account of Mr Erskine's pleas. In the event, the sentence pronounced was one year's hard labour and a recognizance for good behaviour of £1,000. Erskine firmly, if erroneously, believed that if the Society had followed his advice and shown compassion public sympathy would have been aroused and *The Age of Reason* would never again have been published in England.

---

8.   This account is contained in a letter which Erskine wrote to the editor of the State Trials. *Op.cit.*

CHAPTER 11

Conspiracy and Criminal Libel

Uproar in Court

April 1799 saw Erskine again acting in his accustomed role - for the defence. A man named Arthur O'Connor was found not guilty of high treason by the jury on a trial at Maidstone.[1] A new warrant for his re-arrest had already been issued, however, and when, on the acquittal, an officer attempted to serve it a scuffle which erupted into pandemonium ensued in the courtroom. Among those involved in the fracas were the Earl of Thanet, a Whig nobleman, and Mr Cutler Fergusson, a rising young barrister and one of the counsel in the first trial, who later became Advocate General at Calcutta and Judge Advocate to Queen Victoria.

The Tory Government prosecuted these two and others for conspiracy to rescue O'Connor from the custody of the sheriff of Kent - a charge which if proved might well cost

---

1.   Subsequent events revealed that O'Connor was indeed guilty but these were not known to the jury or to O'Connor's friends who at the time included Erskine.

them their fortunes and their lives. The trial took place on April 25, in the King's Bench before the ever-present Lord Kenyon. The equally ubiquitous Erskine for the defence argued that the evidence for the prosecution, including that of various lords, knights and Judges, was not sufficient to prove the case and that the Bow Street Runners who had started the fighting were not to be believed.

He reminded the jury that the Judge had often told other juries that whilst a defendant might in fact be guilty, in law there had to be a preponderance of evidence before they could pronounce a penal judgment. Such a maxim, he said, had given British courts of justice their value in the country and with mankind. But if the courts were so popular and estimable - if they had been through ages upon ages the source of public glory and private happiness - why was this trial to furnish an exception?

It appears likely that there would have been an acquittal if Richard Brinsley Sheridan, who had been so helpful in the trials of Thomas Hardy and Horne Tooke, had not been called to give evidence for the defendants. Sheridan was asked if, from what he had seen at the time, the accused had *assisted* in the escape of O'Connor? Although asked about what he had actually witnessed Sheridan, under severe pressure from prosecuting counsel, finally conceded that he believed they *wished* him to escape, which was a different matter. On re-examination by Erskine, he confirmed that he did not believe that they had taken any part in rescuing O'Connor. But the damage had been done and the jury found all the defendants guilty.

An unusual feature here was that when the accused were brought up for sentence they were allowed to submit affidavits in mitigation. Notwithstanding this indulgence and despite their testimony, the Earl of Thanet was fined

£1,000 and imprisoned in the Tower of London for one year, and Fergusson was fined £100 and imprisoned for one year in the King's Bench prison.

Cutler Fergusson later published a report of the trial in which he expressed his gratitude to Erskine for his efforts on his behalf. "Of his defence", he wrote, "let those who heard it judge. It equalled any of those former exertions by which he has for ever shut out all higher praise ... whom the force of genius and eloquence has raised to a height in his profession where he excites no envy and whose whole life, not untried on the slippery stage of politics nor unexposed to the allurements of corrupt ambition, has been a life of honour, integrity and independence. During a period of 20 years he has fought every arduous contest in which the rights of his countrymen and the cause of general liberty have been involved. So many and splendid have been the triumphs of his eloquence that they have left him no further honours to attain".

The Case of *The Courier*

As we have seen, when Fox's Libel Bill was before the House of Lords it was vehemently opposed by the Judges who declared that it was contrary to common law; in reality Star Chamber law which is precisely why it was introduced into Parliament. Once it was enacted, the Judges shamefully used their position in an endeavour to undermine it. An example of this was revealed in the case of *The Courier* newspaper which the government found anathema and whose publishers were prosecuted for criminal libel before a Special Jury on March 4, 1799.[2]

It was a singular case. The background was an edict passed by the Tsar of Russia prohibiting the export of timber, naval equipment and other goods from his country. This had a serious effect on the commerce of Britain and other countries including Russia itself. *The Courier* merely copied a paragraph which had appeared in several other papers.

This said, "The Emperor of Russia is rendering himself obnoxious to his subjects by various acts of tyranny, and ridiculous in the eyes of Europe by his inconsistency ... in consequence of this ill-timed law, upwards of a hundred sail of vessels are likely to return to this kingdom without freights".

None of the other papers were touched but the Attorney-General filed a criminal information against the proprietor, printer and publisher of *The Courier*. As the facts on which the paragraph were based were accepted as true by the prosecution, Erskine pointed out that the comments upon them were justifiable, and that there was no malicious defamation of a foreign government, only a wish to point out the wrongs done to British subjects.

He also confirmed that since Fox's Libel Act the Judge could not say what was a libel as a judgment of law. The jury were to decide from all the circumstances of the case and they could not find these defendants guilty without plain injustice. He said he spoke with little anxiety for his clients since he had never before had to answer a charge "so completely and manifestly unfounded". In this he was too sanguine since, despite the Libel Act giving the jury the right to decide what was and what was not

2.   27 *State Trials*. 627. 1820.

a libel, Lord Kenyon defiantly told the jury, "I am bound by my oath to declare my own opinion, and I should forget my duty if I were not to say to you that this is a gross libel".

In commenting on the case, Lord John Campbell wrote that the Libel Act only allowed the Judges to give their opinion on matters of law in libel as in other cases. But, he asked, did any Judge ever say to a jury, "Gentlemen, I am of opinion that this is a wilful, malicious and atrocious murder"? Yet, he had heard one Judge declare, "As the legislature requires me to give my own opinion in the present case, I am of opinion that this is a diabolically atrocious libel".[3]

Lord Kenyon appears to have swung the Special Jury who, in spite of Erskine's pleas, returned verdicts of guilty. The Judge then sentenced the proprietor of *The Courier* to six months' imprisonment with a fine of £100, and the printer and publisher to one month's imprisonment each.

Cuthell the Bookseller

Mr Cuthell was a much respected bookseller in London who dealt almost exclusively in classical works. In court, Erskine was to set the scene. He described Cuthell's shop as being in a gloomy avenue of Holborn. It had, he said, "no coloured lamps or transparent shop glasses to dazzle the eye of vagrant curiosity. [And] nothing scarcely is sold which the sun has gone down upon, so in his house nothing almost is to be seen that is not sacred to learning and consecrated by time ..."

---

3.   *Op.cit.* 517.

"There", he continued, "you find the hunter after old editions - the scholar, who is engaged in some controversy, not concerning modern nations, but people and tongues which have for centuries passed away ... Whilst crowds in the circles of gaiety or commerce are engaged at other libraries in the bitterness of political controversy, the pale student sits soberly discussing at Mr Cuthell's the points of the Hebrews or the accents of the Greeks".

In this unlikely shop, on one occasion, without authority, a member of Mr Cuthell's staff sold a few copies of a political pamphlet written by the Rev. Gilbert Wakefield, an eminent if rather eccentric scholar.[4] As soon as Mr Cuthell was aware of this he withdrew the pamphlet from sale. Nevertheless, criminal informations were filed not only against the author and publisher but also against Mr Cuthell for seditious libel.

His case came for trial on February 21, 1799, before Lord Kenyon.[5] The pamphlet contained attacks on the government but Erskine, as counsel for the bookseller, declined to discuss whether or not it was libellous - no doubt because he thought it was. Instead, he argued that Cuthell could not be criminally responsible since he was ignorant of the contents of the pamphlet and the sales had been without his authority. He chose to forget that in a case some years before, when Pitt had been his junior, he had secured an acquittal on a similar argument, only to have Lord Mansfield overrule the decision and direct the jury to convict as a matter of law.

All Wakefield's earlier works had been upon subjects of ancient learning only. But in this case the Attorney-

---

4.   *Reply to the Bishop of Llandaff.* 1798.
5.   *State Trials. Op.cit.* 641.

General indicated that the present book had already been pronounced libellous by Special Juries when two other booksellers, a Mr Johnson and a Mr Jordan, had been tried and found guilty. And, he added, it was clearly established in law that a master was liable when, even without his knowledge, a servant sold a seditious publication.

But why in printing and publishing, asked Erskine, should a man be answerable criminally for the act of his servant when he was not in all other criminal cases? To make it a crime, and inflict a punishment, was shocking to humanity and insulting to common sense.

It was not the rule in civil cases, he explained, and it existed in criminal cases simply because "political Judges, following one another in close order, and endeavouring to abridge the rights and privileges of juries, have perverted and distorted the clearest maxims of universal jurisprudence, and the most uniform precedents of English law".

The Libel Act, said Erskine, lay before him and expressly and in terms directed that the trial of a libel should be conducted like every other trial for every other crime. It further provided that the jury should decide not upon the mere fact of printing and publishing but upon the whole matter including the intention of the defendant. This was the rule by the Libel Act and they, the jury, as well as the court, were bound by it.

However, Lord Kenyon had the last word on the Libel Act once again. He attacked the statute, which he admitted he had opposed in the House of Lords, as resulting from a race for popularity between two seemingly contending parties, who then chose to run amicably together. The fact that it had cross-party support gave it no more merit in his eyes.

The defendant was duly found guilty but the case was

regarded as sufficiently unsatisfactory that after a short spell in prison he was released on paying a fine of 30 marks.

Ultimately, in 1843, Lord John Campbell secured the enactment of a new Libel Act which bears his name and expressly allows a defence in criminal libel cases that the publication was by a servant without authority from the accused.

70,000 Enemies

As for the Rev. Gilbert Wakefield, he was separately charged with seditious libel and took the risky course of defending himself.[6] Wakefield had turned from classical studies to write in his pamphlet that, "Within three miles of the house, where I am writing these pages, there is a much greater number of starving, miserable human beings ... than on any equal portion of ground through the habitable globe".[7] He concluded from this that the labouring classes had little to fear from a French invasion.

Unfortunately for him, the Judge believed that this was an invitation to 70,000 enemies to invade the country. He also claimed that the prisoner's address to the jury had aggravated his offence. Wakefield was found guilty and sentenced to two years' imprisonment which resulted in much public sympathy and a subscription to help him. Nevertheless, after his release, on August 18, 1801, he was writing to a friend about his difficulties in finding accommodation suitable for his family after being in

---

6.   *State Trials.* xxvii. *Op.cit.* 679.
7.   *Op.cit.* 36.

prison.[8] Sadly, as it happened, he had not long to live and died the same year, aged 45, some 14 weeks after serving his sentence.

---

8.   BM. *Add.Mss.* 44,992. f. 156.

CHAPTER 12

The Deranged Soldier

Shooting at the King

On May 15, 1800 the King with Queen Charlotte and their daughters occupied the royal box at Drury Lane Theatre ready to enjoy Colley Cibber's comedy, *She Would and She Would Not*. Suddenly, a shot rang out from near the orchestra and the King was within inches of being killed. However, he kept his presence of mind and refused to leave the box. The man seen holding the gun was seized by a member of the orchestra and taken to the music room below the stage for safe-custody, the audience having become extremely agitated by the attempted murder of the Sovereign.

The would-be-assassin was James Hadfield. Without delay he was examined by the Duke of York, Sir William Addington and Richard Brinsley Sheridan who were all present at the play. On seeing the Duke the prisoner exclaimed, "God bless you; I know you Royal Highness; you are the Duke of York; I served under you". The recognition seemed to be mutual with the Duke remembering him as one of his orderlies. On being questioned Hadfield said he was tired of life and regretted nothing but the fate of his wife.

When he was being taken away Hadfield spoke again, saying to the Duke, "God bless you", and to those around, "He was the soldiers' friend, and the soldiers loved him". Being subsequently brought to trial on a charge of high treason Hadfield chose Erskine as his counsel.

The trial commenced in the King's Bench on June 26, 1800 before Lord Kenyon and three other Judges.[1] In court was young law student John Campbell, later to be Lord Chancellor. He was to write of that day, "Being yet a boy, for the first time in my life I entered the Court of King's Bench and beheld Lord Kenyon. The place where the trial was going on was a small room ... and here were crowded together the Judges, the jury, the counsel, the attorneys, and the reporters, with little accommodation for bystanders". As for Erskine, Campbell wrote that he was amazingly struck by his "noble features and animated aspect".

He also wrote that from the opening of the case by the Attorney-General he formed a very low estimate of the eloquence of the English Bar. "But when Erskine began the defence, he threw me into a frenzy of admiration, and indeed I should have been fit for nothing had I been less excited; for this was perhaps his *chef d'oeuvre*, and, therefore, the finest speech ever delivered at the English Bar".[2]

The Attorney-General, by now Sir John Mitford, opened the case for the prosecution and outlined what had happened at Drury Lane. The fact, he said, of Hadfield firing at the King would be so clearly established that

---

1.   *State Trials. Op.cit.* 1281.
2.   *Op.cit.*

there could be no doubt of his guilt unless the misfortune of insanity were offered as an excuse. In law, he continued, if a man's mind was so diseased that he was incapable of distinguishing between good and evil and was completely deranged then the mercy of the law held that he could not be guilty of a crime. But nothing deprived a person of the ability to distinguish between good and evil except "total absolute debility" of the mind.

That, indeed, is how the common law had stood since the time of Sir Edward Coke and Sir Matthew Hale. Nonetheless, Hale had endeavoured, not very successfully, to distinguish between total and partial insanity, holding that it was total only if a man was like a wild beast. According to Professor Nigel Walker, Hale's exposition was "... to exercise the minds of lawyers, psychiatrists and Royal Commissions for the next three centuries".[3] Sir John Mitford accepted it, however, and promised that the evidence would show that Hadfield did not possess the mentality of a wild animal but had acted as other men would do in similar circumstances.

Witnesses were examined who described the shooting and spoke of the prisoner as a man who on the day had both spoken and acted as a sane person. The Duke of York was then called and as he entered the witness box Hadfield exclaimed in a loud voice, "God Almighty bless his good soul; I love him dearly". The Duke testified as to what had happened when the prisoner had been examined at the theatre. Asked if Hadfield had said anything to make the Duke think his understanding might have been deranged, he replied that on the contrary he had spoken as collectedly as was possible.

The Duke was the first witness Erskine chose to cross-

---

3. *Crime and Insanity in England.* 38. 1968.

examine. Asked how orderlies were chosen for an officer
of his rank the Duke replied that they were taken as the
most tried and trusted men. Had the prisoner been asked,
Erskine queried, how he reconciled his protestations of
affection for the Duke with the firing of a pistol at his
royal father? When he had been asked why he had
committed this act, replied the Duke, he said only that
he was tired of life. Asked if he had given any explanation
of what he meant, the Duke said he had added that he
thought he would certainly be killed if he made an
attempt on the King's life.

When the prosecution evidence was concluded it
appeared that it had established that not only was
Hadfield not a wild beast, but that he had acted with
premeditation. However, it was now Erskine's turn to
address the jury. He first touched upon the "remarkable"
fact that the King had been openly shot at in a public
theatre in the heart of his capital and yet not a hair of
the head of the supposed assassin was touched. And now
he was having the benefit of jury trial with the counsel
of his choice assigned to him by the court. It placed the
country and its government upon the "highest pinnacle
of human elevation".

Madness

Erskine then proceeded to develop the concept of partial
insanity explored by Hale. The invisible line that divided
perfect and partial insanity, he said, was difficult to
define. After all, most felons were under some degree of
partial insanity when they committed their crimes. And
whilst there must not be too great an indulgence given
to great crimes so, too, there should not be a kind of
inhumanity towards the defects of human nature.

Erskine accepted that the Attorney-General had correctly indicated what the great jurists Coke and Hale had laid down as the law on insanity. Nevertheless, he went on, if total deprivation of memory was taken in its literal sense, such as an accused not knowing that he had children, then no such madness ever existed. It was idiocy alone that placed a man in that helpless position. But many insane persons who had been brought before the courts had most perfect memories and often a most remarkable subtlety.

After outlining different kinds of madness Erskine indicated a type in which delusion without frenzy or raving madness revealed the true character of insanity for which a man standing for life or death for a crime should be acquitted. With such delusions,

> the imagination still holds the most uncontrollable dominion over reality and fact; and these are the cases which frequently mock the wisdom of the wisest in judicial trials; because such persons often reason with a subtlety which puts in the shade the ordinary conceptions of mankind; their conclusions are just and frequently profound; but the premises from which they reason, when within the range of the malady, are uniformly false; not false from any defect of knowledge or judgment, but because a delusive image, the inseparable companion of real insanity, is thrust upon the subjugated understanding, incapable of resistance, because unconscious of attack.

Having said that, Erskine made it clear to the jury that the prisoner had not secured a counsel who would carry the doctrines of insanity even so far as the books would warrant. He could not, he said, allow the protection of insanity to a man who only exhibited violent passions. It had to be that a man's whole reasoning and conduct, though governed by the ordinary dictates of reason, proceeded upon something which had no foundation or existence. The accepted maxim that every person who had knowledge of good and evil ought to be responsible for crimes was too general a mode of considering the matter.

Speaking then of Hadfield himself Erskine said to the jury, "Gentlemen; it has pleased God to visit this unhappy man before you, to shake his reason in its citadel; to cause him to build up as realities, the most impossible phantoms of the mind, and to be impelled by them as motives irresistible; the whole fabric being nothing but the unhappy vision of his disease - existing nowhere else - having no foundation whatsoever in the very nature of things".

Unable to do otherwise, Erskine acknowledged that all the prosecution witnesses, including the Duke of York, had said they had seen no signs of insanity in Hadfield on the day of, or at the time of, the shooting. But he believed, he said, he was more in the habit of examination than any of those witnesses including the illustrious Duke of York. He then described his examination for the greater part of a day in that very court of an unfortunate gentleman who had indicted a most affectionate brother for having imprisoned him as a lunatic in an asylum at Hoxton.

Erskine continued that his instructions had left him in no doubt that the man was a lunatic but had not given him a clue as to what his lunacy involved. Hence his every effort to expose the man's infirmity was foiled by the man appearing to be in his perfect senses. Then, he said,

At last Dr Sims came into court, who had been prevented, by business, from an earlier attendance.

From Dr Sims I soon learned that the man believed himself to be the Lord and Saviour of mankind ... I then affected to lament the indecency of my ignorant examination, when he expressed forgiveness, and said with the utmost gravity and emphasis, in the face of the whole court, "I am the Christ". And so the case ended. Gentlemen, this is not the only instance of the power of concealing this malady; I could consume the day if I were to enumerate them ...

He did indeed, however, outline similar cases including one involving an imaginary princess where the accused had learnt from the consequences of his admissions never to mention the fantasy again.

Atrocious Wounds

Erskine then told the jury that the question before them was whether the accused had intended violence to His Majesty or had gone to the theatre dominated by the most melancholy insanity that ever degraded and overpowered the faculties of man.

Hadfield, he continued, was a soldier who served in Flanders under the Duke of York as an orderly for the Duke himself. You would have noted, he said to the jury, how calmly the prisoner had sat during the trial - except when emotion overtook him at the entrance of the Duke. The loyalty he exhibited extended also to the King who never had a more gallant, loyal or suffering soldier. His gallantry and loyalty, he said, would be proved. His sufferings spoke for themselves.

When the British army was attacked near Lisle, he continued to a rapt jury, the unfortunate Hadfield received his first wound. Turning to the prisoner he then placed his hand on his head and said, "You may see the effect of it now. The point of a sword was impelled against him with all the force of a man urging his horse to battle". He (Erskine) had engaged a Mr Cline to examine the prisoner in Newgate and his conclusion was that under the resultant surgery the displaced part of the skull had been taken away or forced inward on the brain.

The second stroke Hadfield received had cut across all the nerves which gave sensibility and animation to the body so that his head was almost severed. Although nearly destroyed the prisoner had continued to fight for his country when a sword divided the membrane of his neck where it met the head and cut into his brain.

Insanity was the instant effect of these wounds, said Erskine, and "to end all further description", the prisoner was then thrust through the body with a bayonet and left in a ditch with the slain. There he was found and taken to a hospital where he was seen to be bereft of his senses by a man who was to be called as a witness. After these dire wounds, counsel continued, the prisoner imagined that he had constant intercourse with the Almighty, that the world was coming to an end, and like Christ he was to sacrifice himself for its salvation. That was the blessed sacrifice he imagined he went to the theatre to perform. It would be his execution for treason.

Erskine then proceeded to indicate other signs of Hadfield's insanity when he had tried to dash out the brains of his eight-month-old child against the wall. He was only prevented from this act by neighbours who restrained him. At the time he had memory. He knew the child was his and tears of affection had run down his face. But he believed that Heaven had told him that the moment he was dead, for killing the child, all nature would be changed and all mankind redeemed. His delusion was that he must be destroyed but should not destroy himself.

Rather surprisingly, in the light of what had gone before, Erskine now felt able to tell the jury that he made no appeal to their passions since they had no right to be swayed by them.

A number of witnesses, including Mr Cline, were then called to testify to the prisoner's insanity. When Elizabeth Roberts, who was Hadfield's landlady, gave evidence of the attack he had made upon his child, Lord Kenyon intervened to ask if Erskine had nearly finished his evidence? Erskine replied that he had 20 more witnesses to examine. Upon hearing this the Judge asked Sir John Mitford whether he could call any witnesses to contradict the facts being put before them?

Insanity as a Defence

If a man, said the Judge, was in a deranged state of mind at the time of committing an offence he was not criminally answerable for his acts. "I confess", he continued, "the facts proved by the witnesses ... bring home conviction to one's mind, that at the time he [Hadfield] committed this offence, and a most horrid one it is, he was in a very deranged state ... It is impossible that this man with safety to society can be suffered, supposing his misfortune is such, to be let loose upon the public. But in a criminal prosecution, I will, in this part of the business, throw it out for your discretion ... whether it is necessary to proceed further".

The Attorney-General replied, "I must confess, that I have certainly no reason to imagine that this is a coloured case ... the circumstances which have now been stated, were perfectly unknown to me". Under continued prompting from the Judge he then decided not to proceed further with the prosecution and agreed with him that though the prisoner should be acquitted he would have to be confined in a suitable place for the safety of society. Normally, at that time, prisoners found to be insane were returned to the care of their families without much regard to their safety or that of the public.

Erskine now rose and addressed the Judge saying, "My Lord, we who represent the prisoner, are highly sensible of the humanity, justice, and benevolence of every part of the court ... Most undoubtedly the safety of the community requires that this unfortunate man should be taken care of".

William Garrow, one of the Crown Counsel, asked if the jury could state in their verdict the grounds on which they based it; namely, that they acquitted the prisoner for insanity at the time the act was committed? There would then be a legal reason for his future confinement.

Having been told by the Judge that if the scales hung anything like even, it was their duty to throw in "a certain proportion of mercy", the jury found the prisoner "Not Guilty, being under the influence of insanity at the time the act was committed". Shortly afterwards a statute was enacted permitting detention during the pleasure of the Crown of anyone acquitted of a felony or treason upon the ground of insanity.[4]

The wording used by the jury continued in use until 1883 when Queen Victoria was shot at by a man who was subsequently acquitted as being insane. The Queen complained that he should have been found guilty, and by an Act of that year it was provided that the formula should be changed to "guilty of the act or omission

---

4.   40 Geo. III. c. 94. (1800).

charged against him, but insane at the time.[5] This, however, obscured the fact that in law the verdict was really one of acquittal from which no appeal was possible. Today the verdict has reverted to "Not Guilty by reason of insanity".

The importance of Hadfield's case was that Erskine had circumvented the normal test of ability to distinguish right and wrong by arguing solely from the premise of Hadfield's clearly established delusion. However, the case, and the ruling of Lord Kenyon, were not generally followed and in 1843 the waters were muddied by the *M'Naghten* Rules laid down by the Judges in response to questions put to them by the House of Lords.

Briefly, these provide, as was the situation before Erskine's brilliant success in Hadfield's case, that it is a defence for the accused to show that he was labouring under such a defect of reason, due to disease of the mind, as *either* not to know the nature and quality of his act *or,* if he did know, not to know that he was doing wrong.

Also at the present time, by s.2 of the Homicide Act of 1957, although mental disorder falling short of insanity is generally no defence to a charge of murder, a verdict of manslaughter must be returned if the accused is found to be suffering from diminished responsibility which can include irresistible impulse. This allows the Judge a discretion as to punishment which is not available in cases of murder. It is of interest to note that in 1978, there was no murder case in which the *M'Naghten* Rules were successfully pleaded by adults in contrast with 78 findings of diminished responsibility.[6]

As for Hadfield, he was committed to Bedlam asylum,

---

5. *Trial of Lunatics Act.* Section 2(1). (1883).
6. *Criminal Statistics.* (Cmnd. 7670).

where the Duke of York visited him and where he outlived George III and all the jurymen, Judges and counsel involved in the case. At the time of the trial he was only 29 years old. When he had become a very old man, Lord John Campbell visited him and found him reading a newspaper and talking very rationally on the topics of the day. Campbell concluded, however, that he continued to be subject to strong delusion at times, and that it would be very unsafe to discharge him from custody.[7]

Erskine's speech to the jury was described by Campbell as, "perhaps his greatest display of genius in defending a party prosecuted by the Crown ... It is now, and will ever be, studied by medical men for its philosophic views of mental disease, - by lawyers for its admirable distinctions as to the degree of alienation of mind which will exempt from penal responsibility, - by logicians for its severe and connected reasoning, - and by all lovers of genuine eloquence for its touching appeals to human feeling".[8]

Erskine himself was pleased to confess to Thomas Howell, the editor of the most distinguished volumes of *State Trials*, that, "None of my speeches have been so much read and approved". Nonetheless, because of the subsequent *M'Naghten* Rules, and despite Lord John Campbell's prognosis, its impact has regrettably been blurred.

7.　　*Op.cit.* 527.
8.　　*Ibid.* 520.

CHAPTER 13

Civil Actions

Attacking the Judge

Before we take leave of Erskine in his profession at the Bar to become Lord Chancellor we can gain some further insight into his extraordinary power over juries; this time in civil cases in which he was briefed. When he went on general retainers he was almost always successful. But first we should look at one case which he lost, for which he never ceased to blame the Judge. This was *Day v. Day* which was heard at the Huntingdon Assizes, before Mr Justice Heath, in 1797.[1]

The issue before the court was whether the defendant, who was heir to a large estate, had in reality been a child purchased from a poor woman in a workhouse. Erskine appeared for the plaintiff and feeling confident of success spoke of the character and conduct of the defendant as being in every way worthy of a genuine descent. He told the jury he would enjoy no triumph or gratification in

---

1.　　*Ibid.* 527.

being the instrument of the justice he sought from them when it would give so much pain to a deserving individual wholly guiltless of the fraud which had placed him in the court.

But he added, it was necessary in equal justice to consider the other side of the case and to be impartial by considering the situation of the plaintiff if the defendant's birth really were as suggested. As the action proceeded the witnesses for the plaintiff did not entirely come up to proof on cross-examination and at the end, after the Judge had summed up, the jury found for the defendant. Erskine must have wondered whether he had not been too self-confident in this instance. But he would not blame himself.

On his return to London he wrote a letter to his instructing attorney in which, apart from praising him for his work on the case, he said: "The charge of the Judge is a reproach to the administration of English justice, being, from the beginning to the end of it, a mass of consummate absurdity, and ignorance of the first rules of evidence. If he had done his duty, I think the verdict would have been otherwise".

Erskine then applied to the King's Bench for a rule to set aside the verdict and, on this being refused, wrote again to the attorney. "My opinion of Mr Day's cause", he explained, "you can scarcely believe to be at all altered; my mind must be indeed shallow in the extreme if any thing which passed in the King's Bench could make any other impression upon it than that of utter contempt for the prejudices of Judges in the blind support of one another's errors. Kenyon's mind is of a size, and, generally speaking, of a character to disdain such a course; but he appears to me to have laid aside his reason in the speech he delivered" in refusing the rule.

Many years later the plaintiff decided to publish an

account of the trial. Erskine asked him to take care not to abridge a syllable of Mr Justice Heath's summing up since the whole would produce nothing but contempt in the mind of the reader.

However, it could work both ways. It has been said that on one occasion old Mr Justice Gould made another strong summing up against Erskine which was largely inaudible and unintelligible to the jury. Counsel nodded to all that was said, leading the jury to believe that the law was in his favour and to deliver the verdict he wanted. Lord John Campbell considered that this was probably a pure invention, as indeed it may have been, but, of course, such stratagems are not unknown to the Bar.

Criminal Conversation

In the case of *Markham v. Fawcett* an action was brought by the Dean of the Cathedral of York who was a son of the Archbishop of York. His allegation was of criminal conversation, which meant adultery with his wife and depriving him of her comfort and society. The defendant was an old friend of the Dean from their years spent together at Westminster School and Oxford University.

Erskine, for the plaintiff, stressed the evil and horrible calamity which had befallen his client from the five year criminal intercourse of his wife. This involved advocate's licence, however, since although adultery was then a civil offence or tort it was not a crime, despite its description.

"He is tortured", Erskine said, "by the most afflicting of all human sensations. When he looks at the children whom he is by law bound to protect and to provide for, and from whose existence he ought to receive a delightful return ... he knows not whether he is lavishing his

fondness and affection upon his own children, or upon the
seed of a villain, sown in the bed of his honour and his
delight".

The former friend, said Erskine, was a midnight robber
who had secured entry into his client's house with
professions of friendship and brotherhood. It was
impossible to heal a wound which struck so deep into the
soul. Damages should be awarded that would have no
parallel in the annals of fashionable adultery since money
recompense in the civil courts was the only remedy the
law gave. His plea proved successful and the enormous
sum of £7,000 was awarded, although the defendant left
the country and it was never paid.

Adultery Cases

Erskine was briefed in most of the adultery cases of the
day and it may have been cases like the last that
encouraged him to support in the House of Commons a
Bill to make adultery an indictable offence. However, on
February 24, 1794 in *Howard v. Bingham* he was counsel
for the defendant and in an extraordinary appeal to the
jury, managed to persuade them to see his client as the
aggrieved party.

The plaintiff was the heir presumptive of the Duke of
Norfolk and the defendant, and adulterer, the eldest son
of the Earl of Lucan, and afterwards himself the Earl.
The lady in the case was a daughter of Lord Fauconberg
and had been formally engaged to be married to the
defendant. On her becoming acquainted with the plaintiff,
however, her parents, to her dismay, broke off her
engagement since the plaintiff appeared to them to be a
better prospect, and it was the plaintiff whom she
subsequently married.

Erskine was in sparkling form. "I have", he told the jury, "the noble Judge's authority for saying that the gist of this action is the plaintiff's loss of the comfort and society of his wife by the seduction of the defendant. The loss of her affection and of domestic happiness are the only foundations of his complaint. Now, before any thing can be lost, it must have existed ... before the seduction of a woman's affections from her husband can take place, he must have possessed her affections".

After promising that every word he uttered would be supported by incontrovertible proofs, Erskine continued:

I will begin by drawing up the curtains of this blessed marriage-bed, whose joys are supposed to be nipped in the bud by the defendant's adulterous seduction. Nothing certainly is more delightful to the human fancy than the possession of a beautiful woman in the prime of health and youthful passion ... While the curtains therefore are still closed on this bridal scene, your imaginations will naturally represent to you this charming woman, endeavouring to conceal sensations which modesty forbids the sex, however enamoured, too openly to reveal - wishing beyond adequate expression what she must not even attempt to express, and seemingly resisting what she burns to enjoy.

Alas, gentlemen! You must prepare to see in the room of this a scene of horror and of sorrow ... you must behold [this noble lady] given up to the plaintiff by the infatuation of parents, and stretched upon the bridal bed as upon a rack, torn from the arms of a beloved and impassioned youth, himself of noble birth, only to secure the honours of a higher title, a legal victim on the altar of heraldry.

Erskine went on to say that he would prove to the jury

that the lady met her bridegroom with sighs and tears of afflicted love for Mr Bingham, and a rooted aversion to her husband. As a consequence she frequently spent her nights on a couch in her own apartment, dissolved in tears. Indeed, she often told her maid that she would rather go to Newgate gaol than to Mr Howard's bed.

His learned friend, said Erskine, had deprecated the power of what he termed Erskine's pathetic eloquence. But he pointed out that if he had such power the occasion forbade its use. After all, Mr Bingham could only defend himself; he could not demand damages from Mr Howard for depriving him of what was his by a title superior to any law which man had a moral right to make. Mr Howard was never truly married. God and nature forbade the banns of such a marriage.

If indeed, continued Erskine, Mr Bingham could as a plaintiff have told the jury how he had been wronged what damages might he have expected? He, Erskine, would have painted the expectation of an honourable union, and would have shown instead the lady in the arms of another, by the legal prostitution of parental choice in the teeth of affection. "Good God! imagine my client to be plaintiff, and what damages are you not prepared to give him? And yet here he is as defendant and damages are demanded against him. Oh, monstrous conclusion!".

But it was not the conclusion of Erskine's speech since he continued for another hour, even warning the aristocracy of the ruin such a mercenary spirit would bring upon them. So powerful an effect did the speech have upon the jury that they resolved to return a verdict in favour of the defendant with heavy damages. Erskine must have glowed with pride. However, the Judge quickly intervened to remind them that no blame attached to the plaintiff who had not been aware of the previous engagement and who was the lady's lawful husband, which the defendant should have respected.

He told the jury that if they believed adultery had been committed they were bound by their oaths to find a verdict for the plaintiff and would not be justified in branding him by awarding trifling damages. In the end the jury did find for the plaintiff, but awarded damages of £55 which was the lowest amount then common in such cases.

Dunning v. Sir Thomas Turton

There exists only a brief report of this case but again it was one of adultery. Erskine appeared for the husband whom he described as being fondly attached to his wife but whom he suspected of infidelity. Again, he dwelt upon the emotions of his client's soul and the feverish agonies of unrelieved doubt. On this he quoted from *Othello:*

Oh, what damned moments tells he o'er,
Who doubts, believes, suspects, yet strongly loves.

But, he declared, when suspicion became certainty and dishonour to the husband was placed beyond doubt, despair overtook him and well might he have exclaimed in the words of the same play:

- "Had it pleased heaven
To try me with affliction; had He rain'd
All kinds of sores and shames on my bare head;
Steep'd me in poverty to the very lips;
Given to captivity me and my hopes,
I should have found in some place in my soul
A drop of patience. But alas -"

It is said that the eyes of the audience filled with tears. However, in what is an imperfect report the verdict in the case is not given.

Also to be noticed are the cases of *Parslow v. Sykes* where Erskine obtained astonishing damages of £10,000 for the plaintiff, and *Baldwin v. Oliver* where for the defendant he persuaded the jury to assess the plaintiff's damages at a derisory one shilling.

It is interesting to note that despite his outstanding success with witnesses, in time honoured fashion Erskine the great lawyer proved to be a poor witness himself. When the famous actor David Garrick was in difficulties in a case in 1798 Erskine as a witness for him spoilt his own evidence by talking too much. And when Arthur O'Connor was tried for high treason, Erskine's misguided evidence on his behalf was convoluted in the extreme and his egotistical garrulity caused laughter in court.[2]

---

2.   27 *State Trials*. 38. 1799.

CHAPTER 14

A Call to Arms

War Weariness

On July 2, 1800, Pitt, using bribery of Irish MPs, finally destroyed the independence of their country and established the Union of Great Britain and Ireland which came into effect on January 1, 1801. Ironically, however, in the first session of the united Parliament at Westminster Pitt was forced to resign after failing to persuade the King to consent to a measure to bring about Catholic Emancipation in Ireland.

The question, the King told Pitt, was beyond the decision of any cabinet of ministers. And at a subsequent royal levee he added his not uncommon blackmailing threat that anyone voting for such a measure would be treated as his enemy. In consequence, Addington succeeded Pitt as Prime Minister and on behalf of a war-weary people negotiated peace with France. After 10 years of war the respite was greeted with illuminations and public rejoicing. The Whigs played no part in the change of Ministry but several of them gave Addington some support in an attempt both to free him from the continuing influence of Pitt and to help secure the peace for which they had long striven.

It was at this time that Addington offered Erskine the post of Attorney-General. As we have seen, Erskine sought the opinion of the Prince of Wales as to whether he should accept but received what was in effect a snub and certainly no advice. He thereupon declined the offer. In explanation he wrote in a letter to a friend, "I am in a lucrative and honourable situation, and I will remain in it till the time comes (if ever it does) when I can vindicate to friends and foes the change in my situation".

Erskine continued to work alongside his Whig friends in Parliament. He voted to approve the Peace of Amiens and spoke in the debate in the House of Commons on their Motion to thank the Crown for the removal of Pitt. Again, he criticized the former Prime Minister for refusing to discuss peace with Napoleon and claimed that his resignation was a "desertion of the vessel of the state when she was labouring in the tempest, and in danger of being dashed to pieces among the rocks which surrounded her". An Amendment to the Motion, to the effect that Pitt deserved the gratitude of the House for his services, was, however, carried by majority of 224 to 52.

War Fever

Taking advantage of the peace, Erskine visited Paris again in the Long Vacation of 1802 to see for himself the new republic. Here he met Napoleon, who was now First Consul for life, but did not enjoy the same reception as Fox. But then why should he? His renown was forged at the Bar whereas Fox was the second most famous statesman in the country as well as being far more amenable than Pitt to the French. It is noteworthy that whilst dining with Fox the First Consul told his guest that he could not bring himself to approve of trial by jury since, "it was so Gothic, cumbrous, and might be so *inconvenient* to a government". Fox boldly responded that, "the *inconvenience* was the very thing for which he liked it".[1]

At another sumptuous dinner for distinguished guests Erskine and Fox were both embarrassed to find that Arthur O'Connor had been invited and was present. O'Connor had lied in his trial at Maidstone which had led to the prosecution of the Earl of Thanet. Erskine as a friend had vouched for O'Connor's political principles only to find that he later confessed to treason and, after being banished by Act of Parliament, had undertaken military service in France. However, unlike Fox, Erskine avoided conversation with him and no incident occurred.

Fox said Napoleon never hid his intentions, and within the year the future Emperor was openly preparing to renew the war and English public opinion veered round to a spate of jingoism. In order to forestall the enemy in his preparations Addington's government now changed direction and declared war against the French Republic on May 17, 1803. This time Erskine supported the government and denounced French warlike actions.

Napoleon made no secret of his preparations to invade England with the fleet he was amassing at Boulogne. And when he arrested every British subject who was in France he further inflamed public opinion in England. Under these circumstances Addington was not the heroic leader the people wanted. His strategy was solely for a defensive war and before long he felt it necessary to resign, with

---

1.   The Rev. George Croly. *The Personal History of His Late Majesty George IV.* 1841.

Pitt returning triumphantly as war leader. Two Militia
Acts were quickly passed and 250,000 men enrolled as
soldiers for home defence as war fever now replaced the
earlier weariness.

Volunteers

Two regiments of the volunteers in London were made up
entirely of lawyers and Erskine was promoted to Colonel
and placed in charge of one of them, known officially as
the Temple Corps. They were reviewed in Hyde Park
before the King who asked Erskine who his troops were.
"They are all lawyers, your Majesty", he replied. With a
humorous chuckle the King suggested that they should
therefore be called, "The Devil's Own", which henceforth
they were.

Lord John Campbell, who was in the other regiment,
the Bloomsbury and Inns of Court Association, wrote that
he heard many stories of Erskine's blunders as Colonel
and thought himself lucky to be under the command of
Lieutenant-Colonel Cox, a "warlike" Master in Chancery.[2]
Erskine was hardly a warlike person however, and it was
many years since he had served in the army.

The volunteers were most likely similar to "Dad's
Army" in the Second World War. Edward Law, later Lord
Ellenborough, who was under Erskine's command, was
said never to have managed to master the difference
between marching with his left or right foot forward. It
was also said in jest that when members of the regiments
were told to prepare to charge they all pulled out pen, ink
and paper and wrote down 6s.8d or 13s.4d.

---

2.   *Op.cit.* 546.

Some time later, when the threat of invasion had passed, Erskine ceased to concern himself seriously with what he called playing at soldiers. Campbell, on the other hand, continued on active service and after the war retained his musket as an heirloom. Other volunteers took a view similar to that of Erskine and wished to retire from their regiments. The government insisted, however, that they must all serve until the end of the war.

This was backed by legal opinion from the Attorney-General and Erskine was formally asked to explain his contrary point of view. He wrote in response that if volunteers were to be indefinitely bound then enlisted soldiers should equally be considered as volunteers and should be equally independent. He believed though that such a doctrine would be both unjust and impolitic and, in any event, that statutes provided for volunteers to retire at pleasure.

As the conflicting opinions were published in the newspapers there was considerable confusion and the matter was actually taken to the King's Bench in the case of *Rex v. Dowley*.[3] The future Prime Minister, Spencer Perceval, (later shot dead in the House of Commons by John Bellingham) and Erskine were briefed on opposite sides and the Judges unanimously decided that the volunteers could resign.

This in turn resulted in a clause being inserted in the government's Volunteer Consolidation Bill to prevent such resignations. Erskine spoke strongly against the proposal. As long, he said, as the country was at war with an enemy, the government could safely trust to the patriotism which had animated the whole population with the desire to fight for freedom. However, once the danger

---

3.   4 East. *Reports.* 512.

of invasion had passed, those who wished to extend their service should be allowed to do so but "do not touch the right of resignation now enjoyed under the solemn judgment of the highest court in Westminster Hall".[4] Subsequently the clause was withdrawn and this success was to prove to be Erskine's last speech in the House of Commons.

Death of Pitt

It was in May 1804 that Pitt had returned triumphantly to office but as it turned out was unable to form a coalition to wage the war as he would have wished since the King still refused to countenance a government containing Fox. Despite this setback Pitt fully intended that the war should now be prosecuted with vigour. But it was not to be. Disasters followed in the war in Europe with the Austrian and Russian armies fleeing before Napoleon's Generals. Then, on January 23, 1806, the ailing Pitt died at the age of 47.

In the Commons his friend, and strong slave trade supporter, William Windham, surprisingly and vainly opposed the address for Pitt's tomb to be placed in Westminster Abbey. In contrast Erskine, who had often suffered the lash of Pitt's tongue and his enmity, voted in favour of the Motion as well as for a public funeral and money to pay Pitt's huge debts. The Common Council of the Corporation of London, disliking Pitt's introduction of income tax, decided to erect a monument to him in the Guildhall by only 77 votes to 71.

Lord Grenville, who had joined the Whigs after leaving

---

4.   1 *Parl.Deb.* 934. 1804.

Pitt over Catholic Emancipation, was now sent for by the King to become Prime Minister. He informed the Monarch that Fox would have to be included in any new government, and for the first time the King agreed.

At this momentous moment for Erskine he suffered the loss of his devoted wife, Frances, after 36 years of happily married life. It was a grievous and tragic blow.

CHAPTER 15

The Woolsack

"Ministry of All the Talents"

Following the death of Pitt the King was obliged to accept the reality that the House of Commons was dominated by Whigs. Greville formed the government but Fox, who became Foreign Secretary, was its leading spirit and organizer. His presence in the government brought about widespread rejoicing. However, there was serious public disquiet when Lord Ellenborough, the Lord Chief Justice, was brought into the Cabinet as this was seen as an unconstitutional breach of the independence of the judiciary. And, despite its name, the Ministry was, in fact, narrowly based. Pitt's followers refused to join and as the new Opposition they provided a good deal of the real talent in Parliament.

Another consequence of the change of Ministry was that the dilatory Lord Eldon was obliged to give up the Great Seal of the Lord Chancellor and difficulties arose in choosing his successor. The post was first offered to Lord Ellenborough. But with a large family to support he preferred the lifelong security of the Chief Judgeship of the King's Bench to the insecurity of the Chancellorship which was dependent on the continuation in office of the government of the day. Sir James Mansfield, Chief Justice of the Common Pleas, was then approached but declined due to his advanced age and to not wishing it to become public knowledge that all his children were illegitimate.

This left Erskine - not an auspicious start for him. Because of Erskine's experience in common law practice Fox had wanted his friend to be appointed Chief Justice of either the King's Bench or the Common Pleas on the elevation of the holder of one or the other to the Woolsack. With the incumbents declining to be elevated, however, this was no longer possible and George III was asked to assent to Erskine as the new Chancellor. The King was none too pleased with the defender of *The Rights of Man* but consented, commenting wryly "Remember he is your Chancellor, not mine".

Baron Erskine

Accordingly, on April 7, 1806 Erskine took up the Great Seal with all due ceremony and was created a peer of the realm as Baron Erskine of Restormel Castle (in the Fowey Valley, Cornwall). This choice of title was in deference to the wish of the Prince of Wales who had inherited the Duchy of Cornwall at birth. For his motto Erskine chose "Trial by Jury", which caused some witticisms as he was now the head of Chancery which knew virtually nothing of jury trial. As a lawyer Lord John Campbell was clearly dismayed at the appointment which he considered to have been made out of political expediency rather than to enhance the work of the Chancery Court.

Others had combined common law and equity practices to some extent but Erskine had never been involved in equity work at all. In an evil hour, wrote Campbell, he yielded to the temptation of "the pestiferous lump of metal" which had proved fatal to so many, and before long he had sunk into comparative insignificance.[1]

However, Joseph Farington, a member of the Royal Academy, noted in his diaries, written from 1793 to 1821, that, "Erskine is likely to make a good Chancellor. He will rise early and labour to prepare himself for a cause. He is also spirited and has resolution".[2]

Perhaps more significantly, Samuel Romilly, who was now appointed Solicitor-General, wrote in his diary that although the new administration had been formed of public men of the greatest talents and highest character some few appointments had been received by the public with much dissatisfaction, particularly that of Erskine as Lord Chancellor.

"The truth undoubtedly is", continued Romilly, "that he is totally unfit for the situation. His practice has never led him into the courts of equity; and the doctrines which prevail in them are to him almost like the law of a foreign country. It is true that he has a great deal of quickness, and is capable of much application; but ... it is quite impossible that he should find the means of making himself master of that extensive and complicated system of law which he will have to administer".

Romilly went on to add that Erskine himself felt his unfitness for the office and had called upon Romilly to ask him what to read and how to make a success of his new office. He had concluded his request by saying, "you must make me a Chancellor now, that I may afterwards make

---

1.   *Op.cit.* 553.
2.   Celia Battersby. "Bench Marks". *Law Society's Gazette.* (December 7, 1994).

you one".[3]

Erskine was, of course, politically and emotionally committed to working with Fox and it was his misfortune that Fox was soon to die and that the Ministry would not survive long without him. Erskine was Chancellor for only 14 months and a similar fate was to overcome Lord Brougham nearly 30 years later. Indeed, Lord John Campbell himself was Chancellor for only two years, although in his case he died in office. The time thus available provided little opportunity for these innovative lawyers to leave the mark on Equity that they would have desired. Lord Eldon, by contrast, sat on the Woolsack for well over 20 years and left behind him a dismal record.

The House of Lords

Erskine made his maiden speech in the House of Peers on a Bill to indemnify witnesses who were to be examined in the forthcoming impeachment of Lord Melville. He is said to have shocked his hearers with his egotism. He told the House that he had been engaged in the duties of a laborious profession for 27 years and this had given him the opportunity of a more extensive experience in the courts than any other individual of his generation. He had been honoured with silk and been engaged in every important cause in the Court of King's Bench. He then immodestly claimed that his experience was not only equal to that of any individual Judge but of all the Judges collectively.

So far as the Bill was concerned Erskine said that on the basis of precedent he would oppose it and he recommended to the House that it should merely declare

---

3. *Memoirs*. ii. 134/5. 1840.

existing law. Despite the shock the speech engendered the
Lords accepted from him an alternative Bill, largely to
that effect, which became law.[4] Whatever his manner on
this occasion it is clear that Erskine wanted to avoid the
danger of witnesses refusing to testify if their civil rights
might be adversely affected.

We have seen that the appointment of the Lord Chief
Justice of the King's Bench, Lord Ellenborough, to a seat
in the Cabinet was not universally approved. In a debate
in the Lords, Lord Eldon and other peers condemned it
on the ground that the Cabinet Minister might, as a
Judge, have to try a prosecution for treason or sedition
which he himself as a politician had recommended and
on the result of which the stability of the government
might depend. Erskine left the Woolsack to support
Ellenborough, expressing the view that the King was
entitled to the advice of all his subjects and that, in any
event, the Cabinet was unknown to the Constitution.

Despite his elevated position in the House, he said, he
would never forget his duty to the people. He would
always remember the active and successful part he had
played in supporting trial by jury and he saw no danger
in the proposed inclusion of the Chief Justice in the
Cabinet.[5] A Motion of Censure was defeated but public
opinion remained unsettled and alarmed.

Erskine next moved a resolution to prevent the
Commons publishing the proceedings in the impeachment
of Lord Melville before the trial was over. In fact, the
proceedings were open to the public and Erskine' position
was clearly contrary to all his earlier pleadings for the
freedom of the press. The Lords duly passed the

4.   Campbell. *Op.cit.* 583.
5.   *Parl.Deb.* vi. 7. 1806.

prohibition and it was accepted by the press but such measures soon became obsolete.

Later, there was a Motion before the Lords to ask the King to remove from the Bench the Irish Judge Fox on the ground of misconduct. Tiresomely, Erskine again alluded to his motto "Trial by Jury", which, he pompously said, ornamented his carriage which was at their Lordships' door and was to be borne, with the insignia of the Erskine family, through all future generations.

However, he repeated that for trial by jury he had fought in the hottest times and should ever fight. On the other hand, it was trial by Judge and jury together which attracted his admiration, so let them proceed against Mr Justice Fox judicially. Not that he had been a flatterer of Judges, he reminded his audience. "Did any man go further to remind Judges of their duties to the country? For my boldness I have received public rebukes, which I have returned I trust with honest indignation".

But in this case, he said, witnesses had complained that the Judge had bullied juries. Yet, in the absence of the Judge, and behind his back, had members of the House not harangued and inflamed one another? Would not all justice perish if such proceedings were sanctioned? If they asked the Commons to impeach they would already have prejudged the man they would be called upon to try. Better to let guilt or innocence be decided by the ordinary courts.[6]

Abolition of the Slave Trade

Fox's greatest triumph when in office was to secure the

---

6.   *Ibid.* vii. 767. 1806.

abolition of the obscene trade in slaves for which he had long worked alongside William Wilberforce and the "Clapham Saints" who had looked in vain to Pitt for solid support. Now the whole power of government was for the first time put behind the crusade for abolition and brought it to fruition. Fox was already seriously ill when he went to the House of Commons to move that the slave trade was contrary to the principles of justice, humanity and sound policy and should be abolished. His Bill was accepted in the Commons by 114 votes to 15. It then passed in the Lords and became enshrined in the law in June 1806, - only a short time before the government expired. It was the culmination of a long, hard-fought battle against an odious and immoral evil.

In the Lords, Erskine supported Fox on the Bill and distanced himself from his own earlier attitude. When he had served in the West Indies, he said, the condition of the slaves had seemed to be comfortable. He had since come to the conclusion that he had been deceived by outward appearances. Man could never be the property of man without evil consequences. The horrors of a slave ship had recently been disclosed to him in the course of his profession. He was proud, he said, that this country was the morning star which was enlightening Europe in destroying the slave trade. It should also set an example of humanity and justice to be followed by all the nations of the earth by abolishing slavery itself.[7]

Death of Fox

Regrettably, soon after, at Chiswick on September 13,

---

7.   *Ibid.* 807.

1806, Charles James Fox died of cirrhosis of the liver at the age of 57. On his death-bed he asked his wife to kiss him. He then said, "I die happy", and, turning back to her added, "but pity you". He had earlier suffered a premonition that he would not long survive Pitt. Erskine had been so perturbed at his chief's decline in health that he had said, "I am so agitated with hopes and fears about poor Fox that my stomach is quite out of order and my spirits flat". Clearly affected, he was one of the pallbearers at Fox's funeral in Westminster Abbey where Fox was buried next to his old adversary Pitt.

Romilly wrote in his diary: "How unfortunate, that so soon after the country had recovered from its delusion respecting him, and was availing itself of his great talents, those talents should be extinguished! ... Most of the persons present [at the funeral] seemed as if they had lost a most intimate, and a most affectionate friend".[8]

Fox had been one of the most colourful and controversial figures of the age. He lived unconventionally but as a statesman he was always guided by humanitarian principles and a belief in freedom. After 38 years' influence on Parliament he was to be sorely missed.

Some time later, Erskine described Fox's truth and vigour and the exuberant fertility of his imagination. When he was called upon to speak unexpectedly, he said, his manner was such that an audience would not anticipate success any more than for a buffalo being approached by a silent snake, "moving slowly and inertly towards him on the grass".

But, "Fox, unlike the serpent in everything but his strength, always taking his station in some fixed invulnerable principles, soon surrounded and entangled

---

8.   *Memoirs. Op.cit.* 170.

his adversary, disjointing every member of his discourse, and strangling him in the irresistible folds of truth".

With Fox it was, "*the heart* which is the spring and fountain of eloquence. A cold-blooded, learned man might, for anything I know, compose in his closet an eloquent book; but in public discourse, arising out of sudden occasions, he could by no possibility be eloquent. "... By contrast the words of Fox rose, "as the lava rises to burst from the mouth of a volcano, when the resistless energies of the subterranean world are at their height".[9]

Judicial Duties as Chancellor

We now leave the political scene and return to the time of Erskine's appointment as Lord Chancellor and his spell on the Woolsack. A meeting of the entire Bar in Westminster Hall had sent him a fulsome message of congratulations. In reply he thanked them for their friendship and paid tribute to the character and honour of the profession. Three days later he rode in great pomp from his house in Lincoln's Inn Fields to Westminster Hall where, accompanied by the Duke of Clarence, afterwards William IV, as well as many peers and privy councillors and all the Judges and King's Counsel, he commenced his career as Lord Chancellor.

With justification, Erskine had always thought that Chancery proceedings were complicated and interminable. On one occasion, Lord Eldon, who preceded him as well as succeeding him as Chancellor, had recommended that one of Erskine's clients who had no common law remedy should apply to Chancery for relief. Erskine had affronted

---

9.   Coly. *Op.cit.* 42/6.

Eldon by asking, "Would your Lordship send a dog you loved there?" This was a corollary to the jest that a dog which could not be confined at home and went about doing mischief should be sent into the Court of Chancery, "for no living thing once there can ever get out again".[10] Shades of Miss Flite's birds in *Bleak House.*

Nevertheless, the Equity Bar treated Erskine with great consideration and he, in turn, acted with all due decorum as was fitting in the "Court of Conscience". On the other hand he did little to improve his knowledge of the principles of Equity, except in so far as was necessary in the cases he presided over.

One such case involved a question of the insanity of a testator. It was not enough, Erskine held in an echo of Hadfield's trial, that morbidity of the mind was alleged to have existed in the past if it was not alleged at the time the will was made. He also distinguished between lunacy and senility, which were deemed the same by some, and pronounced, with all solemnity and for the first time in English law, that the moon had no influence over lunatics - a view not always held today.

Impeachment of Lord Melville

A number of Erskine's judgments turned on the intricacies of the law of real property and trusts and are too involved to be related here. However, he justifiably received a great deal of praise for his handling of the impeachment of Henry Dundas, Lord Melville, in June 1806. Melville had been an ally and friend of Pitt but on April 8, 1805, a Resolution introduced by Samuel

---

10.   Campbell. *Op.cit.* 558.

Whitbread caused his immediate resignation from Parliament and his subsequent impeachment.

Erskine had bitter memories of the impeachment of Warren Hastings (ironically on a resolution by Lord Melville) which had been allowed to drag on in the House of Lords for seven years. On this occasion he was determined that the House of Lords should sit like any other court, that is from day to day until the verdict was delivered.

Accordingly, the impeachment proceedings against Lord Melville lasted only 14 days despite a huge mass of evidence. And Erskine behaved throughout with dignity, firmness and impartiality. The elaborate theatre of the Hastings impeachment was replaced by a well conducted trial. Samuel Whitbread, Sir Samuel Romilly and Serjeant Best appeared for the House of Commons as prosecutors. Sir Thomas Plumer, later an inefficient Vice-Chancellor, and Mr Adam represented Lord Melville.

At one point in the proceedings, seeing that Sir Thomas Plumer appeared fatigued after speaking for several hours, the Chancellor observed, "If you seek for a resting place in a cause so complicated and extensive as this, you may freely choose it for yourself. The court, which ought to be an example to all other courts, will ever hold in the highest reverence the indulgent character of British justice". For which Plumer thanked him profusely.

The charges against Melville arose from his handling of public funds whilst he was treasurer of the Royal Navy. It was notorious that prior to his appointment the treasurer had always handled such funds with great laxity. For instance, one treasurer had left office taking with him £27,000 which was never recovered. It was alleged against Melville that things had not changed as they should have done during his term of office. Indeed, that he had fraudulently converted £10,000 and refused to tell the House of Commons what he had done with it.

His paymaster, Mr Trotter, was said to have drawn huge amounts of navy funds from the Bank of England and deposited them in a private bank in order to buy stocks. Melville merely observed that he had not known what Trotter was doing with the money although he assumed he was making some profit from it. In fact, Trotter had used it to increase his fortune by a staggering 30 times. But, said the loyal Trotter, all detailed matters relating to the accounts were left to the paymaster and Melville had no knowledge of what he had been up to.

For the defence, Plumer argued that if it were a crime, and a violation of virtue and honour, for a public officer to use monies in his hands for his own profit then the most honourable families, and most respectable persons in the kingdom had spent their lives in violating the law and constantly failing in their duty. In which there was undoubtedly a great deal of truth.

The Lords decided to ask the Judges if withdrawing public funds from the Bank of England and depositing them in a private bank was a crime? The Judges answered that it was not criminal to do so. They were then asked if it was a crime for a treasurer to make use of public funds after receiving a salary in lieu of all other payments. Again they replied that it was not. So much for the public morality of the time.

There were no histrionics in the trial and one prosecutor went out of his way to pay tribute to Erskine, saying that, "the noble person presiding in the court has so concentrated all the learning upon the law that the other great legal characters [among the Lords] have entirely gone with him upon every point which has been decided; and not only so, but that all the feelings of propriety, all the judicial dignity, all the mildness towards the defendant, and all the sternness towards the prosecution, which ought to exist in order to cast a restraint upon improper zeal, have likewise appeared to centre in that noble person; so that if there has been wanting a model of trial by impeachment, in all essential points, I think I may venture to say, such a model is now afforded".

At the end of the trial, the peers voted to acquit Melville of all the articles of impeachment. He then made a low bow to the Chancellor and withdrew.[11] Lord Brougham was later to write that there was but one opinion in and out of the legal profession on the great merits of Lord Erskine's admirable conduct in the case.

Nevertheless, despite the undoubtedly favourable reception he received on the impeachment, estimates of Erskine's general role on the Woolsack were not so sanguine. Romilly, who it must be remembered probably sought the Chancellorship himself and, despite his many virtues, could be very disagreeable, later wrote that the existing Tory Ministry would not remain long in power and if those they had supplanted should recover their authority, the Great Seal could scarcely again be entrusted to the hands of Erskine. Despite all Erskine's very great talents, he wrote, his incapacity for the office was too forcibly and too generally felt for him to be placed in it again.[12]

Delivering Up the Great Seal

In the following year of 1807 a Bill was introduced into Parliament to allow Catholics to hold commissions in the

---

11.   *State Trials.* xxix. 549.
12.   *Memoirs.* iii. 394.

army in England to the same extent as Pitt's Irish Act of 1793 had allowed them in Ireland. This was up to, and including, the rank of colonel and was intended to remove inconveniences that arose when Irish troops moved to England. Erskine opposed it but did not consider it necessary to resign. It was a curious measure for the government to have introduced, knowing that Pitt had lost power as a result of the King's abhorrence of "weaknesses" in dealing with Catholics. And Pitt had been the trusted friend of the King which could not be said of any of the Whig leaders. So repugnant did the King find the Bill on this occasion that he insisted the government should drop it and give him a written and signed promise that they would never again propose any measure which would relax the penal laws against Catholics.

Erskine was entrusted with the task of trying to persuade the King to see that the pledge he wanted was unconstitutional. At his meeting with the Monarch he started badly by breaching Court etiquette in raising a matter which the King had not mentioned first. He recounted to Romilly how he told the King that he knew His Majesty had been prejudiced against him but hoped his loyal service had removed that sentiment.

He urged that on the Catholic Bill he thought exactly as the King himself did, but that to ask the Ministers to give a pledge not to advise the Crown on measures which the state of public affairs might render necessary was to involve them in what was almost an impeachable offence. The King, he pressed on him, was on the brink of a precipice. To dismiss his Ministers would cause rejoicing amongst Catholics and he would never know another hour of peace or tranquillity.

The King was clearly agitated by all this and when Erskine had concluded he merely said, "You are a very honest man, my Lord, and I am very much obliged to you". Romilly recorded that the Chancellor thought he had made a great impression and half flattered himself that the King would withdraw his demand.[13] In reality, however, the King took no notice except that he became even more firmly intent on securing a new administration.

And that is what happened. The death of Fox had been disastrous for the "Ministry of all the Talents" and in March 1807 the government was dismissed. Erskine was then summoned to attend the King to deliver up the Great Seal. That morning he attended court and informed the lawyers present of the situation and thanked them for the kind, honourable and liberal manner in which they had conducted themselves towards him. The Attorney-General responded in kind.

In fact, Erskine was permitted to remain in office for a further week to wind up the business of his court. Two days before he parted with the Seal, however, he broke with his former practice of refusing to avail himself of the usual patronage of Chancellors by giving places to his friends and relatives, and appointed his son-in-law, Edward Morris, to be a Master in Chancery.

Romilly thought this most improper, not in itself since it was the normal practice but on the ground that Erskine was supposed to be out of office. Additionally, he thought Morris was unqualified for the post and that the action would draw reproach on the whole administration.[14]

Erskine was never to reconcile himself to losing the Chancellorship in such a summary manner. He later complained to the House of Lords that although the King had the legal right to change his Ministers, if they had

---

13.　*Op.cit.* 194/5.
14.　*Ibid.* 198.

consented to his demand he would have been directly in violation of the Constitution. Moreover, their dismissal for declining to give the pledge was a declaration to Catholics that the penalties and disabilities from which they suffered were considered to be an indispensable part of the law. What the result of that might be he was afraid to contemplate. At all events a "No Popery" government was duly sworn in and Lord Eldon commenced a 20 year grip on the Great Seal with serious adverse consequences.

It was often believed that most of Erskine's decisions as Chancellor were reversed on appeal. This was not so but it led to a curious incident. Two citizens of the United States gambled a quantity of port on the point and one of them, a Senator, wrote to Erskine with some indelicacy to ask him to determine the bet for them. Erskine replied, on November 13, 1819:

I certainly was appointed Chancellor under the Administration in which Mr Fox was Secretary of State, in 1806, and could have been Chancellor under no Administration in which he had not had a part; nor would I have accepted, without him, any office whatsoever. I believe the Administration was said, by all the *Blockheads* to be made up of all the *Talents* in the country.

But you have certainly lost your bet on the subject of my decrees. None of them were appealed against, except one, upon a branch of Mr Thelluson's will - but *it was affirmed* without a dissentient voice, on the motion of Lord Eldon, now Lord Chancellor. If you think I was no lawyer, you may continue to think so. It is plain you are no lawyer yourself; but I wish every man to retain his opinions, though at the cost of three dozen of port.

P.S. To save you from spending your money upon bets you are sure to lose, remember, that no man can be a great advocate who is no lawyer. The thing is impossible.[15]

A Cup Too Many

On a personal note, Joseph Farington recorded in his diaries that at one of the Lord Mayor's Easter feasts, Lord Chancellor Erskine, "got drunk, and rolled about, holding Dignum, the singer, by the arm".[16]

Similarly, on another occasion, not mentioned by Farington, whilst making a speech as counsel for the East India Company, Erskine was drunk after dining too well with the Prince of Wales.

On the same occasion, however, Pitt made one of the worst speeches of his career whilst suffering from a massive hangover.[17] Readers of Creevey's letters will recall that at the time excessive drinking was all too common at the court and amongst the country's leaders. Certainly, it had no serious effect upon Erskine's popularity and Farington also noted that in 1814, "Nollekens was still making marble busts of Erskine priced at 150 guineas: half price if in plaster".[18]

15.   Campbell. *Op.cit.* 597.
16.   Celia Battersby. *Op.cit.*
17.   John Ehrman. *The Younger Pitt.* 454. 1969.
18.   Celia Battersby. *Op.cit.*

CHAPTER 16

Ex-Chancellor

Politician Again

Once he had ceased to be Chancellor at the age of 57 Erskine was not permitted to return to the Bar, but he did receive the statutory pension of £4,000 a year for life. Although still a Member of the House of Lords, he wrote to a friend that he was now retired - most probably for good - and was living an idle but not useless life. If he was unable to return to public duties, he said, he would occupy himself in cultivating the grateful earth which was more reliable in distributing its favours than courts or Princes. In fact, he continued to take an interest in public affairs and to speak in the House of Lords.

The "Government of All the Talents" had been elected by a majority in the country and their measures had been accepted by the Lords. Having been unseated in an unconstitutional manner they miscalculated that their stay in the wilderness would be short-lived. Accordingly, on their behalf on April 13, 1807, Lord Fortescue introduced in the Lords a Motion that in future Ministers of the Crown should not be prevented by a pledge from giving any advice to the King which circumstances required.

As was to be expected, Erskine spoke in the debate in support of the Motion. With something akin to special pleading he decried the fashionable view that the late administration was guilty of an act of political suicide by introducing the Catholic Bill. He would not agree that it was a rash, useless and wanton measure, lacking expediency, and opposed by insurmountable obstacles.

Nor could he accept that the Ministers had practised deception. That was easy to invent, he said, but why should persons of acknowledged skill and ability as statesmen suddenly conduct themselves so absurdly. Why would distinguished integrity suddenly give place to dishonour and falsehood?

Outlining what the Bill had involved he went on to say he could never discover any just or rational ground for the dismissal of the Ministry. The illegality of the pledge asked for by the King was a childish truism, utterly unfit for debate in Parliament. He believed the fate of the Ministry had been decided upon by secret advisers of the King, as indeed was the case.

In political life, he continued, they all knew there were wheels within wheels - as many almost as in a silk mill - some of them sunk so deep in dirt that it was difficult to find them. It had also to be remembered that by the coronation oath the King swore to govern his people according to the laws and customs of the realm. To require of his Ministers a pledge not to give him counsel on any subject was manifestly contrary to the Constitution and the laws and customs of the country. To say, therefore, that the King, without an adviser, was the author of that demand was to say that he had broken his coronation oath.

On this last point, Romilly confided to his diary with

some surprise that no notice was taken of it by any of the peers who spoke after Erskine.[1]

In concluding, Erskine, who had never liked the Catholic Bill, confirmed his Protestant credentials and said he considered the Roman Catholic faith to be a gross superstition - nct chargeable to the present generation which contained thousands and tens of thousands of sincere and enlightened persons - but the result of the darkness of former ages.[2]

Notwithstanding the speeches of Erskine and his colleagues, the Motion was defeated by 171 to 81 votes. Even more shattering to the deposed Ministers was the vote on a similar Motion in the House of Commons where the Whigs had counted on a secure majority. "While we were locked out in the lobby", wrote Romilly, "we supposed ourselves the majority by about 20, but there was a majority of 32 against us".[3] The fate of the Whigs was sealed. Although he does not say so directly it appears from Romilly's full account that it was very likely that a number of Members did not relish the opportunity of deciding with Erskine that the King had broken his coronation oath.

In the same session Erskine spoke in support of the Scotch Judicature Bill which aimed to introduce trial by jury into Scotland. Once again his egotism and vanity got the better of him. He could not refrain from reminding the House of his devoted attachment to that mode of trial and his manner caused some amusement in which the Duke of Cumberland (afterwards King of Hanover) joined. Erskine was furious and made himself more ridiculous

---

1.   *Op.cit.* ii. 203.
2.   9 *Parliamentary Debates.* 353. 1807.
3.   *Op.cit.* 201.

by saying:

> I observe an illustrious personage on the benches opposite smile, and I must be bold to tell him that such a smile is inconsistent with the decorum with which this House is in the habit of hearing every noble Lord express his sentiments. But it is particularly indecorous and indecent in that illustrious personage, to smile at a panegyric upon the trial by jury. Trial by jury placed the present royal family on the throne of England, and trial by jury has preserved our most gracious Sovereign, that illustrious person's father, throughout a long and glorious reign. Trial by jury is the best security for your Lordships, and of every order in the state, and I can never cease to feel that trial by jury has enabled me to address your Lordships upon equal terms with the highest man among you.[4]

Soon afterwards, the Parliament was dissolved and following the ensuing General Election the Whigs found themselves in a minority. With ill-judged tenacity, in the new session Erskine vainly returned once more to the role of the King in the dismissal of the former Whig government and declared that Ministers should yield to Parliaments, not Parliaments to Ministers. But he was heavily defeated and henceforth played a much smaller role in debates.

He did, however, oppose a Bill introduced by Sir Vicary Gibbs, by now known as "Sir Vinegar", to enable the Attorney-General to arrest anyone against whom he had filed an *ex officio* information for libel. This was directed at the proprietors and printers of newspapers which

---

4.   9 *Parliamentary Debates*. 487. 1807.

attacked the government. Erskine tried to show that the Bill was unnecessary, that it was a dangerous innovation, and that it was intended to prevent public discussion of grievances. But again he was defeated.

Animals' Rights

Erskine now began to devote himself to the welfare of animals. He introduced into the Lords a Bill for the prevention of malicious and wanton cruelty to animals, saying that it was a subject very near to his heart. Disgusting outrages, which he said were too painful to describe, were being perpetrated upon animals whilst the law did nothing. This was because animals were considered only as property. They were entirely without protection from cruelty and they had no rights. Yet man's dominion over them was not given by God for their torture but as a moral trust.

Nature had provided the same organs and feelings for enjoyment and happiness to animals as to man - seeing, hearing, feeling, thinking, the sensations of pain and pleasure, love, anger and sensibility to kindness. Such creatures might have been created for man's use but not for his abuse. Towards them, as in all other things, men's duties and interests were inseparable. Extending humanity to animals would have a most powerful effect on men's moral sense and upon their feelings and sympathies for each other.[5]

When the speech was published as a pamphlet its editor suggested in the Preface that it should be introduced to families and schools and deserved to be

---

5.   14 *Parliamentary Debates.* 553. 1809.

circulated "among the lower classes of society by the clergy, and by all moral and pious persons".[6]

When the Bill was in its Committee stage Erskine pointed out that during his 30 years of parliamentary life he had never before proposed any alteration in the law. He still had no wish, he said, to link a statute with his name; he had a better motive. If the Bill were enacted it would not only be an honour to the country but would mark an era in the history of the world.

The Lords found no difficulty in accepting the Bill but it received a different reception in the Commons particularly with the speech of William Windham, a turncoat in politics and bitter opponent of any mitigation of the cruel penal code of the time.

What a figure of fun they would all be, said Windham with some logic, if they endorsed a string of commitments under the Cruelty to Animals Bill and then read of statesmen and princes attending a race in which only five out of 50 horses survived, and when the "rights" of foxes were violated with impunity. He then alleged that Erskine was thinking of himself and not the interests of the community at all. And he sneered, that for Erskine to be the first who stood up as the champion of the rights of brutes was, indeed, a marked distinction. In the event, the Commons proved not to be ready for animal rights and the Bill was defeated.[7]

Refusing to be discouraged, Erskine reintroduced his Bill in the next session of the Lords with some amendments. Learning, however, that when it reached the Commons it was likely to be defeated again he withdrew it after it had passed in Committee. Later, to

---

6.   Published by Richard Phillips. 1809.
7.   17 *Parliamentary Debates*. 1207. 1810.

his great satisfaction, it was introduced in the Commons itself where, with Windham no longer present, it was accepted and after passing through the Lords was enacted as Statute 3, Geo.4, c.71.

Parliamentary Privilege

In the same year of 1810, Erskine again supported an extension of rights for Catholics. At the same time Sir Francis Burdett, MP for Westminster, was committed to the Tower by the House of Commons for reflecting on its privileges in denouncing as illegal its sending a radical to Newgate.

Burdett at first refused to surrender to the House and barricaded himself in his house in Piccadilly. Lord Cochrane then drove up in a coach, pushed a barrel of gunpowder through the door, and prepared to mine all entrances and defend Burdett with arms. So many people thronged the streets in support of Burdett that a riot threatened to spark and this led him finally to submit. The affair caused Erskine to urge that all questions of parliamentary privilege should be determined by the common law courts and not by the Commons.

Deciding issues of parliamentary privileges was not a power sought by the common law courts, however, and would clearly have been unconstitutional. Nevertheless, recalling that in 1689 the House of Commons had sent Chief Justice Pemberton to Newgate for an alleged breach of privilege, Erskine exclaimed that if a similar attack were made on Lord Ellenborough he would resist it with all his "strength and bones and blood".[8]

---

8.   16 *Ibid.* 851. 1810.

Also at this time Romilly was conducting his crusade, against powerful entrenched opposition in the House of Lords, for the reform of England's notorious "Bloody Code" of penal law under which well over 200 offences attracted the death penalty. Perhaps Erskine saw small chance of success against the settled attitudes of the Lords. But it is little to his credit that only once did he vote in favour of Romilly's Bills and then when he was one of a small minority who wanted to make stealing in a shop to the value of five shillings non-capital.

On a more personal note, at this point Erskine wrote a letter to Lord Hardwicke supporting the publication of the manuscripts of Hardwicke's grandfather (a former Lord Chancellor) whom Erskine described as "so truly great a Judge" who enjoyed a "great reputation". He also urged that the editing should be entrusted to a Mr Pepys.[9] Of Lord Chancellor Hardwicke it was said that as great a multitude would flock to hear him as to hear Garrick. And Lord Mansfield held that he owed all his success to Hardwicke's example.[10]

Prince of Wales Deserts the Whigs

By now George III was found to be incurably mad and anticipation of office grew among the Whigs on the prospect of their political ally, the Prince of Wales, becoming Regent. These included Erskine who was still on terms on intimacy with the hitherto Whig Prince. Accordingly, he opposed the power of electing the Regent which the two Houses of Parliament had adopted earlier

---

9.   BM. *Add.Mss.* 35,648. f. 304. January 24, 1810.
10.   John Holliday. *Life of Lord Mansfield.* 105/6.

when the King was temporarily insane and Pitt had feared for his government. Such an election, declared Erskine, was inconsistent with an hereditary monarchy as the heir apparent was entitled to become Regent by right of birth.[11]

As it happens the Prince of Wales was again elected Regent but rudely shattered the expectations of the Whigs when he found that after all his true interests lay with the Tories and kept them in office. The Prince not only embraced his old enemies but completely turned his back on his former friends and became as determined as his father had been to see that they did not achieve power.

11.   18 *Parliamentary Debates*. 72. 1810.

CHAPTER 17

Semi-Retirement

Leisure Pursuits

No longer at the apex of public life Erskine began to
devote himself to the life of a man about town where his
happy temperament and humour, his gaiety and his wit
were much enjoyed by his friends. As one of them put it,
"His spirits were lively, his disposition for frolic and fun
in private society so extraordinary that to those who were
strangers to him it was impossible to believe that he was
the celebrated Mr Erskine or anything else but a
schoolboy broken loose for the holidays".[1]

As we shall see, he continued to involve himself in the
larger issues of the day but it was in the courtroom that
his star had sparkled brightest. And it is significant that
during his "retirement" he was rarely mentioned in the
diaries of Creevey and Croker who chronicled the
important political and social occasions of the time.

In his private life he was sometimes overtaken with

---

1.   Lord Abinger. *Op.cit.* 64.

melancholy. However, he continued to frequent the theatre and, on June 30, 1812 he wrote a letter to Mrs Siddons full of praise for her performance on stage the previous evening.[2] Indeed, he had earlier acknowledged his debt in his own eloquence to the harmony of her periods and pronunciation. He also found time to write a letter to Lord Liverpool requesting a situation as Assistant at the Newspaper and Pamphlet office in Somerset House for a young man named Samuel Brewer who, with a large family, was in reduced circumstances.[3]

He still had his villa at Hampstead and a letter Erskine wrote to a J. Dunnett on November 1, 1808, contains a rough sketch he drew of his freehold and leasehold lands around the house which adjoined Kenwood Lane on the road to Highgate close to the famous "Spaniard's" Inn. It appears from the letter that he was likely to lose some of the land when a lease fell in and he was hoping to replace it by buying an adjacent field from the new Lord Mansfield.[4]

He frequently gave parties at the villa and we have a record of one of them, held on January 23, 1808. This was portrayed in the diary of the discreet Romilly who wrote that among those present were the Duke of Norfolk, Lord Grenville, Lord Grey, Lord Holland, Lord Ellenborough, Lord Lauderdale, Lord Henry Petty, Thomas Grenville, Sir Arthur Pigott, William Adam, Edward Morris and himself. "A great Opposition dinner", Romilly called it.

An American Minister, Mr Pinkney, was also there, to the dismay of Romilly who thought the Opposition should not identify themselves with America. However, he

---

2. BM. *Add.Mss.* 45,880. f.1.
3. *Ibid.* 38,275. f. 129.
4. *Ibid.* 29,475. fol. 77.

appears to have been satisfied when politics were hardly mentioned. Erskine seems to have amused the company by talking about his regard for animals and, in particular, those to whom he was attached.

Peculiar Pets

These included a favourite dog which he took to all his consultations when in Chambers, and another dog he had rescued from some boys in the street when they were about to kill it. The first, a large Newfoundland dog called Phoss, was taught to sit upon a chair in Chambers with his paws placed before him on the table. Erskine would put an open book before him, a wig upon his head and one of his advocate's bands around his neck. What his clients thought of this exhibition we do not know but it is unlikely that they would have forsaken him for another counsel. On March 2, 1811 he sent a bitch to a fellow peer with a note to say that, "her name is *Lucky* and may all good luck attend your Lordship".[5]

He also had a pet goose which followed him about in his grounds, a macaw and a great many other dumb friends. He even had two special leeches which he believed had saved his life when he was ill and which he called his "bottle conjurors". These he kept in a glass and, he said, he gave them fresh water every day and had formed a friendship with them. He would often argue the likely result of a case on how they swam or crawled.

Erskine said he was sure they both knew him and were grateful to him. They were called Home and Cline after two celebrated surgeons with quite different dispositions.

---

5.   *Ibid.* 35,649. fol. 125.

After some conversation about them at the party Erskine produced the leeches in their glass which he placed upon the table. It was impossible, however, wrote Romilly, "without the vivacity, the tones, the details, and the gestures of Lord Erskine, to give an adequate idea of this singular scene."[6]

It was in Hampstead that Erskine could relax and from where he wrote to Dr Samuel Parr, "I am now busy flying my boys' kites, shooting with the bow and arrow, and talking to an old Scotch gardener 10 hours a day about the same things, which, taken all together, are not of the value or importance of a Birmingham half-penny, and am scarcely up to the exertion of reading in the daily papers".

Manufacture of Brooms

Later, in consequence of his reduced means, Erskine had to sell the Hampstead villa. In its place he acquired a small estate in Sussex which produced nothing but stunted birch trees and proved a disaster. Rather surprisingly, to reduce his loss arising from the purchase he commenced manufacturing brooms. One day one of the men he employed to sell them about the country was arrested for doing so without a licence under the Hawkers and Pedlars Act.

On his salesman being taken before a magistrate, Erskine went in person to defend him and argued that there was a clause to meet the case. Asked was it was, he replied, "The *sweeping* clause, your worship - which is further fortified by a proviso that, 'nothing herein contained shall prevent or be construed to prevent any

---

6.   *Op.cit.* ii. 239/41.

proprietor of land from vending the produce thereof in any manner that to him shall seem fit"'.

In order to improve the estate Erskine began to study farming and requested the assistance of the famous Coke of Holkham who figured so largely in the Agrarian Revolution. Erskine quipped that, "having been instructed by Coke at Westminster, I am now to be instructed by Coke, as great a man in his way, at Holkham". But the great agriculturalist was not so sanguine about his pupil, remarking that when Erskine had come to a finely cultivated field of wheat, the first example he had seen of drill husbandry, he had exclaimed in delighted tone, "What a beautiful piece of lavender!".

About this time Lewis James, an attorney of Gray's Inn, asked Erskine for his legal Opinion on the case of a Mr Russell. Russell had sold his home in England and was travelling to America to live when he was captured by a French privateer and imprisoned in France. On his subsequent return to England his agent, seemingly without his knowledge, purchased some land for him in Normandy. Erskine wrote on November 3, 1812, that, since the country was at war with France, the government would prosecute a British subject for high treason under statute 33 Geo. III 27 for such a transaction. However, he believed that on the facts of the case proper representation would secure a pardon and he recommended that one be sought.[7]

Humour in Court

A different estate was involved when Erskine appeared

---

7.   BM. *Add.Mss.* 44,992. f. 156.

for a plaintiff seeking to recover the deposit he had paid for a house he wished to purchase on the strength of an advertisement by the auctioneer James Christie of Pall Mall. The house was described as having an extensive and beautiful lawn, with a distant prospect of the Needles in the approaches to the Solent, and an excellent billiard room. To show how his client had been deceived by Christie's rhetoric Erskine resorted to humour.

Going down, he said, to this earthly paradise his client had found nothing to correspond with what he had been led to expect. There was a house but it was falling down and even the rats had left it. It was in a commanding situation since it commanded all the winds and rains of heaven. There was no lawn, only a small yard. But there was a dirty lane close by and Mr Christie might contend that there had been an error in printing so that for "lawn" should be read "lane".

But where, continued Erskine, the plaintiff asked in an agony of disappointment, was the billiard room? "At last he was conducted to a room in the attic, the ceiling of which was so low that a man could not stand upright in it, and therefore must perforce put himself into the posture of a billiard player. Seeing this, Mr Christie, by the magic of his eloquence, converted the place into a 'billiard room'. But the fine view of the Needles, gentlemen; where was it? No such thing was to be seen, and my poor client might as well have looked for a needle in a bottle of hay!" The jury found for the plaintiff.

Of course, Erskine rarely resorted to humour in state trials where the lives of the prisoners were at stake. But it was used to good effect for his clients in less serious cases, such as that above.

On another occasion, an action was brought by a man who, whilst travelling in a stage coach which started from an inn called the "Swan With Two Necks", had been

thrown and had his arm broken. "Gentlemen of the jury",
said Erskine, "the plaintiff in this case is Mr Beverly, a
respectable merchant of Liverpool, and the defendant is
Mr Wilson, proprietor of the 'Swan With Two Necks' in
Lad Lane - a sign emblematic, I suppose, of the number
of necks people ought to possess who ride in his vehicles".

In a case where Erskine was appearing for the
defendant, who this time was the owner of a stage coach,
the plaintiff, a Mr Polito, who kept wild beasts in the
Exeter Exchange, was suing for the negligent loss of his
portmanteau. Having sat in the front of the coach with
his luggage on top, Erskine asked, "Why did he not take
a lesson from his own sagacious elephant and travel with
his trunk before him!".[8] Poor Mr Polito lost his case to
the chagrin of Lord Kenyon who had directed the jury to
find in his favour.

Regrets

Erskine often remarked on how deeply he missed his
work at the Bar and when he became a Bencher of
Lincoln's Inn he frequently dined nostalgically in the Hall.
He was duly flattered when a group of young barristers
asked him to include in his Protection of Animals Bill a
clause to protect *juniors* because they had suffered a great
deal of bad treatment since he had left the Bar. He, no
doubt, also missed his income at the Bar since he had
informed Wilberforce in 1796 that he had received 66
special retainers of 300 guineas each at least, and the
number had increased to nearly 100 before his elevation
to the peerage.

---

8.   William Townsend. *Twelve Eminent Judges*. 437. 1846.

His disappointment at having also to leave the Woolsack was plain when a navigator, on being asked upon what he had lived when frozen up at the North Pole, replied that he and his companions had lived upon seals. And very good living too, interrupted Erskine, "if you keep them long enough". At another party, held on a lawn, he approached a monkey which had a long white hairy mantle flowing gracefully over his head and shoulders and to the amusement of bystanders said, "Sir, I sincerely wish you joy - you wear your wig for life".[9]

Gretna Green

As a result of the war with America in 1812, Erskine's securities there became valueless. He also lost the money he had invested in the estate in Sussex and, beset with financial difficulties, he not only bemoaned the sale of the villa he loved in Hampstead, but had to give up his fine house in Lincoln's Inn Fields and go to live in a smaller house at 13, Arabella Row, Pimlico.

Then, when aged 68, he married a former domestic servant named Sarah Buck who appears to have domineered over him even, said Brougham, knocking him down in front of his son.[10] According to evidence she gave in court after Erskine's death, Sarah had lived with Erskine for some years before they married and had borne him two children.[11]

Apparently he had promised to marry her and, in October 1818, they travelled to Gretna Green where the

---

9.   Campbell. *Op.cit.* vi. 621.
10. Letter to Creevey. *Op.cit.* January 17, 1815.
11. *The Times.* (July 12, 1826).

wedding took place and, according to Scottish law, the two children became legitimate. Erskine's eldest son followed the couple in an endeavour to prevent the marriage taking place but Erskine foiled him by disguising himself in an old woman's dress. Perhaps uncertain about the law in the land of his birth, Erskine also held his cloak over the children during the ceremony since tradition had it that only in this manner could true legitimacy be assured.

Three years later another child was born to the couple whom they named Hampden, after the celebrated opponent of the illegal Ship Money taxation of Charles I. When the infant was about a year old Erskine penned a sonnet to him in a letter to his esteemed friend Dr Samuel Parr. It ran:

Thy infant years, dear child, had pass'd unknown,
As wine had flown upon thy natal day;
But that the name of Hampden fires each soul,
To sit with rapture round thy birthday bowl -
Honest remembrance of his high renown
In the great cause of law and liberty.

Should Heaven extend thy days to man's estate,
Follow his bright example; scorn to yield
To servile judgments; boldly plead the claim
Of British rights, and should the sacred flame
Of eloquence die in corrupt debate,
Like Hampden, urge their justice in the field.

"These last lines", he added, "may one day get this young gentleman hanged, unless he can take one just turn in hanging very many who so richly deserve it".[12]

---

12.   *Letter to Dr Parr*. February 17, 1822.

In his will, Dr Parr left his friend a mourning ring as a mark of his "unfeigned respect for his noble exertions in defending the constitutional rights of juries and the freedom of the press, and for his vigorous and effectual resistance to the odious principle of constructive and accumulative treasons".

Erskine's family consisted in all of eight children, four girls and four boys. One of the girls, Frances, became the wife of Dr Holland, Prebendary of Chichester and her sister May married the Edward Morris whom Erskine appointed a Master in Chancery. The son David became a Minister to the USA. Henry took religious orders, whilst Thomas was appointed a Judge of the Common Pleas. Esme Stewart was a soldier who died from severe wounds at Waterloo by the side of the Duke of Wellington to whom he was adjutant-general. What became of Hampden remains a mystery.

Author

About this time Erskine published a romance which he called *Armata*. It was intended as an allegory in the manner of More's *Utopia* and Swift's *Voyage to Laputa* but, since it lacks their power of ideas and universal appeal, it has not survived as they have. The narrator in the book is shipwrecked and finds himself on another planet with various regions named "Armata" for England, "Patricia" for Ireland and "Capetia" for France. The first part of the book deals with the politics and history of England and the second describes the manners and customs of London life.

The great patriot of Armata is Charles James Fox and Erskine goes to great lengths to suggest that if the French Revolution had been treated differently by foreign nations its excesses would not have been provoked and war might have been avoided. Indeed, as in the early stages of the Revolution France sought to negotiate, this might well have been the case if the counsels of Fox had been heeded or if he had been granted an opportunity to carry them into effect.

The narrator also refers to the significance of the State Trials of 1794 in Pitt's reign of terror. He comments that it was inimical to the Constitution for the government to stamp accusations against individuals with its supreme authority when inferior tribunals were afterwards to judge them. Nevertheless, in any other nation, he remarks, the consequences to the accused would have been fatal; but there was a talisman in Armata which, whilst preserved, would make her immortal, "- HER COURTS OF JUSTICE SPOKE ALOUD TO HER PARLIAMENT; - THUS FAR SHALT THOU GO, AND NO FARTHER".

Erskine suggests in the novel that Judges should wear clothing of distinction when out of court and he discusses economic issues but without revealing any understanding of the new thinking of Adam Smith. And he concludes with an argument for the immortality of the soul. The book was popular enough to go through several editions before it finally fell into neglect.

Erskine also published a booklet entitled, *Defence of the Whigs* which caused a fluster of opposing pamphlets to which he replied with his own *Answer*. His arguments caused near apoplexy in Francis Place who was politically astute and could be a deadly enemy. Place prepared a lengthy reply in his notebooks but it was never completed or published since as the Whigs were out of office at the time he considered it not worthwhile proceeding with.

In response to Erskine's attack upon him in the *Defence*, Place retorted that whilst he had recognized

Erskine's "eloquent, learned and manly exertions during the State Trials in 1794", he now thought him "contemptible" in defending the Whigs.[13] But that is what Erskine had always done!

The "Six Acts"

The end of the war with France after Waterloo brought severe economic distress to the working people of Britain. The "remedy" of the government to the rising agitation this provoked was another bout of coercion. Habeas Corpus was again suspended and a Seditious Meetings Bill introduced. In the House of Lords Erskine denounced these measures as likely to excite discontent rather than allay it and as being injurious to the Constitution.

Of the new Bill he said, "If the authors of this Bill had the government of the seasons, they would no doubt set about a reformation upon their own system and the elements of fire, water and air would no longer have their immemorial liberties, but would be put under such politic restraints as we are now about to lay upon the civil world".[14]

August 1819 saw the "Massacre of Peterloo" in which 11 persons were killed and many hundreds injured when yeomanry attacked a peaceful demonstration in Manchester with drawn swords. Ignoring a great public outcry, the government congratulated those responsible and hurried through Parliament the repressive "Six Acts".

These gave magistrates fresh powers to convict political

---

13. Place's reply is to be found in BM. *Add.Mss.* 35,154, ff. 2-86. *Francis Place Papers.* lxxxv. 1819.
14. 35 *Parliamentary Debates.* 1224. 1818.

opponents of the government summarily without the delays involved in prosecutions at Assizes. They were authorized to search private houses, as well as places of public resort, to confiscate weapons, to suppress all drilling and training in the use of arms (which was sound policy) and to close any meeting they chose. Penalties against allegedly blasphemous and seditious publications were strengthened and the heavy newspaper tax was extended to all periodical journals.

The debates in Parliament on these measures were stormy and Erskine took a keen part in them. In strong terms he condemned the "massacre at Manchester" as well as the government's approval of it without holding any inquiry. He went on to say:

I have had many more opportunities of knowing the sentiments and feelings of those who are classed as seditious subjects than most of your Lordships can have had, and it is my unalterable belief that a system of alarm, supported by mysterious green bags and the array of special commissions, followed as they have been, and will be, by convictions sufficiently numerous to inspire terror - not sufficiently numerous to enforce subjugation - only exasperate evils, the unfortunate existence of which we all deplore. The present discontent may be silenced by severity, but it will be a dangerous silence ...

Confide yourselves in the people and all murmurs and discontents will be at an end. For my own part, while I have life and strength to raise my voice, I will continue to protest against them here and everywhere. I will not repeat with the same oath what I swore in the House of Commons when similar restrictions were in agitation, but I will say firmly, that I was born a free man and I will not die a slave.[15]

As the several Bills were brought forward Erskine opposed each one of them at every possible stage but they were all enacted.

Then, on January 29, 1820, the now totally mad George III finally died after 59 years on the throne and the Prince of Wales became King, as George IV. This led to the saga and trial of his Queen, Caroline.

---

15.   41 *Parliamentary Debates*. 441. 1819.

CHAPTER 18

The Trial of Queen Caroline

The Delicate Investigation

Widely mocked as "The Prince of Pleasure", as a young man the Prince of Wales lived a life of luxury and debauchery. In consequence, it was the ardent wish both of his parents and the government that he should marry and settle down. That he had already secretly, and illegally, wed the Catholic Mrs Fitzherbert he kept a closely guarded secret.

To overcome his reluctance to a royal marriage the Prince was told that in return his huge debts would be paid and his income increased by about £40,000 a year. On the strength of this undertaking he married Princess Caroline of Brunswick, on whom he had never set eyes, in 1795. In fact, she was extremely slovenly and a notorious shrew, and the Prince hated her from the first moment he saw her.

Indeed, the feeling was mutual but the Prince was considered to have behaved the more badly when a year after their marriage he sent Caroline and their few-months-old baby, Princess Charlotte, to live apart from him. As a result the public began to sympathize with their future Queen.

By 1806 Whig Ministers in the "All Talents" government, who felt beholden to the Prince for helping to secure office for them, were concerned about rumours that Caroline had borne an illegitimate child. They quickly carried the gossip to the ears of the Prince who sought advice from Romilly. He drew up a statement setting out what the rumours consisted of and Erskine (who was Lord Chancellor at the time) read it to the King.

On the suggestion of the King a Committee of the Privy Council, including Erskine, was then set up to inquire into the allegations. Its probing became known as "The Delicate Investigation". After examining many witnesses the Committee sent a Report to the King signed by Lords Erskine, Spencer, Grenville and Ellenborough on July 14, 1806. They informed him that they were perfectly convinced there was no truth in the rumour that Caroline had borne an illegitimate child but that there was some evidence of relationships formed by the Princess which were disturbing. However, although George III expressed some disquiet, he was not disposed to pay much attention to the Report and remained a good friend to the Princess.

When the Prince of Wales eventually became Regent and dropped his Whig friends in 1820, he found that in a tit-for-tat mood they were now more disposed to side with Caroline who was demanding to have her honour redeemed and to take her lawful place beside her husband. Forcefully separated from their daughter, Princess Charlotte, she had now become the darling of the people and Henry Brougham and Samuel Whitbread were engaged to act as her legal advisers.

"I really felt, as did Whitbread", Brougham wrote later, "that the conduct of the Prince had been such from the beginning towards his wife, and his later treatment of both mother and daughter so outrageous, as made it a duty to take their part; whilst his conduct towards the Whig party made this proceeding on our part quite justifiable, and not at all inconsistent with our party connexion".[1] In fact, Brougham used the opportunity to play politics although his devious behind-the-scenes manoeuvres caused consternation among his colleagues. These were unknown to the general public, however, where his fame grew apace.

Ultimately, suffering from great indignities at the hands of the Prince, Caroline left England for the continent on August 14, 1814. Whilst she was residing in Italy her enemies collected a dossier against her alleging misconduct which, in 1819, was handed to the Prince who, seizing his chance, immediately resolved to divorce her. As we have seen, on January 29, 1820, George III died. The Prince, now George IV, sent the dossier to both Houses of Parliament and ordered the drawing up of a Bill of Pains and Penalties as a means to prosecute the Queen for adultery. This contained a clause to deprive Caroline of her title of Queen and another to annul her marriage to the King. She, in response, appointed Brougham to act as her Attorney-General.

Prosecution of the Queen

The trial before the House of Lords was set for August 17, 1820. By then London was in a frenzy of delirious excitement and support for the Queen with huge crowds thronging the streets with flaring torches and filling craft upon the river. Shouts of "The Queen! The Queen!" rang

---

1.   Brougham. *Historical Sketches*. ii. 169.

out everywhere. In ale-houses toasts to the health of the King's enemies were drunk by soldiers and the government began to fear bloody revolution. Castlereagh, who lived next door to the house in St James's where the Queen resided during the trial, moved out all his belongings and had his house shuttered for the duration.

The case was purely a political act and there was no necessity to prove guilt beyond reasonable doubt as in a criminal trial. However, Brougham made a brilliant opening speech and his peroration pleading for mercy and justice for the Queen had Erskine rushing from the House in tears.

When he had sufficiently recovered, Erskine, who was now 70 years of age, returned and rose from his place to declare that the proceeding was so rare and anomalous that no precedent could be found to apply to it. The Queen, he said, had to contend against the Crown and its Ministers and all the powers and influence which they possessed. And, unlike most cases of treason, here the King was personally involved and was the accuser.

"It is a criminal charge against the Queen", added Erskine, "or it is nothing. Yet it has none of the precision which is the very characteristic of English law. Her Majesty is not charged with any specific act of adultery, but with 'an adulterous intercourse' - and this not at any specified time or times, but during her whole absence from England, for six years altogether ... This unparalleled generality of accusation creates an unparalleled difficulty of defence and renders a list of witnesses indispensably necessary to the ends of justice".

After dealing with the Queen's sufferings and praising the profession of the law, Erskine asked for her the same rights as ordinary citizens had in the lower courts. To deny her these, he pleaded, would cast a shadow upon England's fame, and he asked the Lords to remember that the powers they had were held in trust. If the Queen were denied the protection of the law they would deservedly be treated like sentinels who deserted or slept at their posts.

An analogy between the Bill and a trial for high treason, he continued, arose from the punishment to be inflicted on conviction.

What, my Lords, he cried, is death, which in a moment ends us, to the lingering and degrading suffering, which the accused may, under our judgment, be sentenced to endure? Born a Princess of the same illustrious house as the King her consort, and now raised to wear the imperial crown of the greatest nation that ever flourished on the earth, - she may be suddenly cast down to shame and sorrow - and not only excluded from the society of her exalted kindred, but for ever deprived of the esteem and affection of the whole female world. For my own part, my Lords, this appears to me the heaviest and most intolerable punishment which any human tribunal can inflict.

Despite this passionate plea, and many more in Erskine's speech, he was defeated upon a division of the House by 78 votes to 28.[2]

At intervals Erskine continued to intervene in the drawn-out proceedings, always attempting unsuccessfully to secure for the Queen the details of the charges against her and a list of the prosecution witnesses. When some of these witnesses had given their evidence Erskine examined it at length and exposed to the Lords what he called disgusting instances of fraud and perjury. At one

---

2.   *Hansard.* Various cols. 1820.

point he was taken ill and the House adjourned. But he found the will to resume his speech two days later.[3]

When the Attorney-General proposed a postponement of the proceedings to enable more witnesses for the Crown to arrive from abroad Erskine strenuously resisted the suggestion. He even went so far as to say he would resign if such a proposal were accepted in the face of all precedent. Fortunately, the clamour from the public for justice for the Queen was proving so intense that the Attorney-General withdrew his request.

Brougham's Triumph

Brougham now audaciously took the initiative by obliquely suggesting that he held in reserve the secret of the King's illegal marriage to Mrs Fitzherbert, the disclosure of which would have meant his abdication. Brougham then proceeded to tear to shreds the flimsy evidence of many prosecution witnesses.

The nation rocked with laughter when witnesses from Italy, and in particular a trusted servant of the Queen named Theodore Majocchi, constantly replied to Brougham's penetrating questions with the words, *"Querto non mi ricordo"* (I don't remember). Referred to by *The Times* as "Signor Non Ricordo", Majocchi, and other witnesses who joined in the refrain, lost all credibility. Reluctantly, the government recognized that it was defeated and announced that it would not send the Bill to the House of Commons.

Erskine spoke of his rejoicing to see the odious measure rejected. "My Lords", he said, "I am an old man, and my

---

3.   *Ibid.* 1469.

life, whether it has been for good or for evil, has been passed under the sacred rule of law. In this moment I feel my strength renovated by that rule being restored. The accursed charge wherewithal we had been menaced has passed over our heads. There is an end of that horrid and portentous excrescence of a new law - retrospective, oppressive and iniquitous. Our Constitution is once more safe".[4] This was to prove to be Erskine's swan song in the House of Lords.

After her acquittal the Queen travelled in triumph to her home on the banks of the Thames near Hammersmith amidst tumultuous throngs of frenzied people. Many houses on the route were illuminated with candles, glimmering gaslights, huge initials "C.R.", stars and imperial crowns. Such scenes of intense rejoicing lasted several days with an estimated one million people expressing spontaneous joy.

In keeping with his conduct throughout, the King decided to prevent the Queen attending his coronation in Westminster Abbey where she was rudely turned back at the door. His continuing dilemma was resolved, however, when Caroline unexpectedly died on August 7, 1821. Accompanied by Brougham, her body was conveyed to Germany, where she was buried in the family vault in her native Brunswick.

---

4.   *Hansard.* iii. 1747. 1820.

CHAPTER 19

Return to Scotland

The Butler's Ghost

After his stand for Queen Caroline, and therefore against his old friend the King, Erskine was once again a favourite of the people. He was loudly cheered when he appeared in public, the freedom of corporations was showered upon him and prints and busts of him adorned countless homes.

As another expression of this esteem, he was invited to a public dinner in his honour in the still proud city of Edinburgh. He accepted with alacrity as he wished to visit again the Old Town of his childhood and see for the first time the splendour of the New Town built on fields he had known well.

Since his childhood the loch which previously had formed the northern boundary of the city had been drained and the valley turned into an extensive public garden at the foot of the Castle rock, separating the Old Town from the New. The showpiece of the new Georgian part of the city was Charlotte Square at the west end laid out by Robert Adam.

Full of nostalgia, however, Erskine found he preferred the old to the new. He visited his former homes and schools and at one point returned to a close where he was convinced he conversed with the ghost of the old family butler. Here he claimed that coming out of a bookseller's he found the old man looking, "pale, wan and shadowy as a ghost". Asked what he was doing there the butler had replied that he wanted to meet Erskine to seek his help in securing some money that was due to him. He then vanished.

As a boy Erskine had often visited the flat of the butler in the Old Town and he now went there to see the old man's widow. She informed him that on her husband's death-bed he had told her that the Earl's steward had wronged him of some money and that, "when Master Tom returns, he will see you righted". Claiming that the impression of the ghost was indelible on his mind Erskine recovered the money due and paid it over to the widow.

The Welcoming Banquet

Because of the trial of Queen Caroline, feelings ran high between the Tories and the Whigs in Edinburgh. Accordingly, the Tories decided to boycott the reception for Erskine who was perceived to be an enemy of the King. Amongst others, Sir Walter Scott refused to meet him. Nevertheless, the dinner, held on February 21, 1821, was an outstanding success with all the leading Scottish Whigs doing honour to their guest. His forensic triumphs were recalled, he was enthusiastically toasted, and he was frequently reduced to tears.

In his after-dinner speech Erskine dwelt upon his admiration for the land of his birth. "The great Author of our nature", he said, "has implanted in us all an instinctive love of our country. It is this which makes the heart throb and vibrate when the eye recalls even the inanimate scenes of our earliest youth". That is why he would enjoy the highest pleasure in visiting the places of his young days.

He dwelt at length on the glory which the Scots had acquired by their love of country and said that however they might be driven to seek their fortunes in the most distant countries, they remained eager to return to their own. Not that he himself had appeared to be so eager at any earlier time.

He concluded by saying, "I shall look back with delight on this day during the remainder of my life - a period which cannot now be much prolonged - and I hope that all who shall ever be descended from me will hold it in perpetual remembrance". One person who was present wrote to Lord John Campbell to say, "It was a light, rambling and jocular speech - whereas our stock speakers deliver on such occasions regular and formal spoken *Essays*".[1]

The Thistle

Campbell also records that a "prejudiced" Mrs Grant of Laggan wrote of Erskine in Edinburgh. "The party have been paying great homage to Lord Erskine, and talking of his return to Scotland after 51 years' residence [in England] as if a comet had reappeared. I was asked to meet him last Saturday night, and saw him surrounded by all his satellites. He is a shattered wreck of a man, decked with a diamond star. This decoration he wore, I

---

1.   *Op.cit.* 660.

was told, as a Knight of the Thistle. I always thought of him with the deep straw bonnet which he wore on his Gretna Green expedition".

The decoration had, in fact, been bestowed on Erskine some years before by the Prince of Wales as a mark of esteem to his friend "Tom". He wore it more frequently than was wise and replied to jests against him that, although the Order of the Thistle was a distinction for the nobility of Scotland, he had never departed from his well-known principles and friendships.

In response to one critic, he remarked, "I will not suffer even a squib to come across the unsullied path of my public life without publicly treading it out". At one time, however, contrasting its green sash with Erskine's inactivity in the House of Lords, Romilly called him "The Green Man and Still" and for a while this became a common name of country inns. Incidentally, Campbell pretended to know nothing of the story about Gretna Green.[2]

Whilst in Edinburgh Erskine also took the opportunity to visit the Court of Justiciary. Here he heard a case which revolved around the question of how far the Judges should go in punishing comments on their own proceedings. A schoolmaster in Glasgow had apparently written to a newspaper a letter disapproving of a judgment of the court. The Scottish Lord Advocate complained that the letter was a contempt of court for which the schoolmaster should be committed to prison.

Counsel for the accused argued that the letter had not infringed the bounds of legitimate discussion and that, in any event, the case should be determined by a jury in the ordinary course of the law. The Judges disagreed,

---

2.   *Ibid.*

however, and proceeded to pass a sentence of imprisonment. Since he had been sitting on the Bench in an honorary capacity, Erskine declined to comment in public, but privately he expressed his regret that in Scotland trial by jury should be disregarded so easily.

He also went to the theatre to see *The Heart of Midlothian* played. Sir Walter Scott was also present and the newspapers wrote that they were both loudly cheered on their separate entrances and departures. But Scott would still not acknowledge Erskine and, since Erskine was more loudly applauded, he wrote in a fit of pique that Erskine's applause had been orchestrated.

Return to London

Before he had time to visit all the places he wished to see, Erskine had to return to London for a huge public dinner given to celebrate the acquittal of Queen Caroline.

He then resumed his private life and, at one point, recalled Burke calling to see him at Hampstead shortly before Burke died. "Come Erskine", said Burke, "let us forget all! I shall soon quit this stage, and wish to die in peace with everybody, especially you". Erskine reciprocated the sentiment and as the once good friends walked in the grounds of the house Burke pointed to the sunset in the sky and remarked in jocular tones, "Ah, Erskine, you cannot spoil that, because you cannot reach it - it would otherwise go - yes, the firmament itself, you and your reformers would tear it all down".

Despite this renewal of friendship, Erskine could not help saying that Burke's speeches in the House of Commons drove everyone away, as indeed they often did. The content, of course, was usually magnificent but not the delivery which was didactic. On one occasion when he emptied the House, continued Erskine, "I wanted to go out with the rest; but was near him, and afraid to get up, so I squeezed myself down and crawled under the benches like a dog, until I got to the door without his seeing me - rejoicing in my escape". However, not all of this was meant to be taken literally.[3]

The Greek Revolt

In 1821 Greece rebelled against its occupation by Turkey. In response, on Easter Day of that year the Turks murdered the Greek Patriarch and three Archbishops in their Cathedral. Shortly afterwards they murdered or took into slavery three-quarters of the inhabitants of the island of Chios. British opinion was shocked and Lord Byron, who joined the struggle, lost his life from fever in the cause of Greek freedom.

Erskine, in support of the Greeks, and with his love of liberty still vibrant, published a pamphlet entitled *Letter to Lord Liverpool*, the then Prime Minister. Erskine, like Byron and many others, harked back to the glory of Greece and was consumed with hatred at the thought of the Turks occupying the sacred land. This feeling was widely held and the atrocities were real enough. Erskine argued that his ink must have become blood to enable him fitly to express his detestation and abhorrence of the Turkish oppressors.

It also led him to remember his conversion to abolition of the African slave trade as he now recalled what had

---

3.   This meeting and these remarks about Burke are referred to in the journal of a Mr Rush, an American Minister, who met Erskine at a dinner at the Duke of Cumberland's.

once slipped his mind. After describing the horrors of the slave ships with slaves jumping overboard only to be eaten by sharks, which he said he frequently saw, he proudly spoke of holding in his hands, when Chancellor, the great charter of their freedom. No wonder, he said, he retained the whole subject of slavery in his mind.

Illness and Death

By the year 1823 Erskine was contemplating returning to Scotland again. This time he wanted his visit to be more leisurely and he also wanted to see his relatives including his brother, the Earl of Buchan. In the autumn of that year, therefore, he decided to spend the winter there. He chose to go by sea rather than face a 400-mile journey in a stage coach, and embarked at Wapping with one of his sons. Off Harwich, he was taken ill and was so indisposed by the time the ship reached Scarborough that he had to be taken ashore.

He recovered partially and managed slowly to reach the residence in Scotland of the widow of his dead brother Henry, twice a former Lord Advocate of Scotland. Here the Earl joined him.

Despite the care and attention he now received Erskine suffered a relapse and died of pneumonia on November 17, at the age of 73. He was interred with a private ceremony in the family burial-place at Uphall, a remote parish in the County of Linlithgow. His estate at the time of his death was small and his widow had to undertake needlework to keep body and soul together and apply to the court to oblige the family to give her some assistance.[4]

---

4.   *The Times. Op.cit.*

CHAPTER 20

Appraisals and Tributes

Invincible Orator

Following Erskine's death the *Morning Chronicle* published a lengthy obituary which it described as an essay of his life. It spoke of the purity of his motives, the brilliance of his talents, his genius and his integrity.

Erskine, it continued, loved Liberty and laboured for it. But to him it was not a mere indefinite notion. Freedom, he had said, was "that which grows out of, and stands firm upon, THE LAW - which is not only consistent with, but which cannot exist without, public order and peace; and which, cemented by morals and exalted by religion, is the parent of that charity, humanly and mild character, which has formed, for ages, the glory of this country".

The paper quoted approvingly from Lord John Russell's *Treatise on the English Government and Constitution* that Erskine's "sword and buckler protected Justice and Freedom; and, defended by him, the government found in the meanest individual whom they attacked, the tongue of Cicero and the soul of Hampden; an invincible orator, and an undaunted patriot".[1] A fitting tribute indeed.

Erskine's interment, despite his fellow-countryman Robert Burns calling him "a spunkie Norland billie", was a sad end to a remarkable life which should have earned him a resting place in Westminster Abbey, alongside Pitt, Fox and Wilberforce. But his fame in history is assured. He never wavered from his principles or party. He is considered by many to be the most glittering advocate and brightest ornament the English Bar has ever known, or may ever know. This is in part attributable to the issues of liberty on which he fought but without his skills and wizardry as a defence advocate they would have counted for little under the onslaught of Pitt's government.

Vanity

Like all of us, however, Erskine had his faults. In some respects he was limited by the prejudices of his age and his party. But his most serious failings were his vanity and egotism. Nevertheless, it must be admitted that these were encouraged by his successes and by the nature of his profession, both of which ensured that he should constantly receive public applause. In any event, he had the facility often to turn his pride against himself so that he was generally laughed at and forgiven. As William Townsend put it,

> With an appetite for applause equal to that of which the celebrated Garrick was accused, he saw the evidences of his triumph daily, and was intoxicated with the incense. The loud laughter or tears of the

---

1.   BM. *Add.Mss.* 39,873. f.57.

audience, the occasional faintings in the boxes, could not more delight the soul of the modern Roscius, open to all the titillations of vanity, than did the visible emotions of jurymen - their relaxed muscles at the jest - the dark look of indignation at the invective - the plaudits, scarcely suppressed in deference to the court - the favourable verdict - gladden the heart of the sensitive orator. Both were alike players, strutting their hour upon the stage, and would alike enact their parts over again, too frequently *encore* their best things at private rehearsals, making their homes a theatre, and their friends an audience.[2]

Nevertheless, his egotism was open to ridicule. *The Morning Chronicle* "apologized" for breaking off the report of a speech of Erskine's at a public dinner. It left many words imperfect and put in a note of apology saying the printers were out of little i's and that all the great I's had been exhausted long before. He was satirized as "Baron Ego of Eye, in the County of Suffolk" and Gillray's caricature of him bore the legend, "Counsellor EGO. - ie, little i, myself i".

William Cobbett wielded his pen to write that in three weeks' time he would have the extreme satisfaction of laying before the public a brief analysis of a speech by Erskine in the House of Commons, his printer having entered into a commitment to furnish a fresh fount of I's.

Byron complained that having sat next to Erskine at dinner he wished trial by jury could be abolished. As he had read his published speeches, he complained, there was no occasion to repeat them to him. At another time,

---

2.   *Op.cit.* i. 458.

however, Byron testified to his enormous admiration for all that Erskine had done for justice. "Anything in his handwriting", he confided to his diary, "will be a treasure, which will gather compound interest for years".

Erskine's vanity also showed itself when he went into the country on special retainers. He would examine the courtroom the night before the trial to select the most advantageous place from which to address the jury. When his case was called he would keep his audience waiting for a few minutes before appearing in a particularly smart wig and a pair of new yellow gloves.[3] But such artifices were not unusual at the time.

Eloquent for Freedom

More importantly, although Erskine could sometimes be overbearing and bully rival counsel and even Judges he won his way into the hearts of juries. And, in any event, when he adopted an overbearing stance it was always struck in the interests of his clients and often of the country if he was to defeat government plans to stifle liberty.

He was passionately partisan, learned in the law and eloquent. He understood what went on in the minds of ordinary people and had the key into those minds when they were to be found in the jury box. His speeches were described by the *Edinburgh Review* as "the most perfect examples of the eloquence of the Bar which are to be found in any age".[4]

As Townsend again put it, "The dervise in the fairy

---

3.   E.S. Roscoe. *The English Scene in the Eighteenth Century.* 390. 1912.
4.   *Op.cit.* 103.

tale, who possessed the faculty of passing his own soul into the body of any whom he might select, could scarcely surpass Erskine in the power of impersonating for a time, the feelings, wishes, and thoughts of others".[5] Lord John Campbell felt delight from the sweetness of his language. The rhythm of the Indian Chief, he wrote, was more varied, richer and more perfect than that of any passage from any other composition in our language.[6]

Espinasse, a law reporter who often saw Erskine in court, wrote that his "action was always appropriate, chaste, easy, natural in accordance with his slender and finely-proportioned figure and just stature".[7]

Henry Roscoe thought all Erskine's speeches had their own great leading principle which, founded in truth and justice, gave them an air of honesty and sincerity which juries found it difficult to resist.[8]

And Lord Holland, who was the nephew of Charles James Fox, wrote that he considered that few lives had been more useful to the laws of the country and to the liberties of mankind than that of Erskine. His successful genius had saved the country from a system of political vengeance and persecution as merciless, although in the opposite direction, as Robespierre's. He thought his speeches at the Bar were models of forensic eloquence abounding in beauties.[9]

James Scarlett, later Lord Abinger, wrote that "As an advocate no language can exaggerate his merits. Cautious, wary, astute, clear in his discernment, and almost infallible in his judgment, no point that could

---

5.   *Op.cit.* 434.
6.   *Op.cit.* 681.
7.   *Ibid.* 425.
8.   *Lives of Eminent British Lawyers.* 1830.
9.   Sir Henry Holland, Bart. *Recollections of Past Life.* 1872.

really serve his client was unobserved, no topic that could advance his cause omitted". He went on to add that Mr Justice Chambers had said that a day at Nisi Prius was very dull unless Erskine was engaged in it; when present he always made it entertaining by his wit and imagination.[10]

Sheridan used to say of his friend that, "Erskine in his gown and wig has the wisdom of an angel, but the moment he puts them off he is nothing but a schoolboy".[11]

For Lord John Campbell, Erskine commanded a love and respect that he could not extend to some other Lord Chancellors about whom he wrote in his *Lives*. "... listen to his discourses", he exclaimed, "when he is rescuing from destruction the intended victim of an arbitrary Government, or painting the anguish of an injured husband, and he appears to breathe celestial fire".[12]

With these personal details, satirical comments and tributes we can glimpse the essential elements of Erskine's orations in the crucial State Trials of the 1790s. And it is to those that we should return in order to appreciate his great distinction as the most outstanding advocate champion of justice and liberty in English history.

Who better to summon up a true vision of this illustrious advocate than Samuel Taylor Coleridge when he wrote:

---

10.   Peter Scarlett. *Memoir of Lord Abinger*. 64/5. 1877.
11.   Quoted. *Ibid.*
12.   *Op.cit.* 680.

To the Honourable Mr Erskine

When British Freedom for a happier land
Spread her broad wings, that fluttered with affright,
ERSKINE! thy voice she heard, and paused her flight
Sublime of Hope! For dreadless thou dids't stand
(Thy censer glowing with the hallowed flame)
An hireless Priest before the insulted shrine,
And at her altar pour the stream divine
Of unmatched eloquence. Therefore thy name
Her sons shall venerate, and cheer thy breast
With blessings heavenward breathed. And when the doom
Of Nature bids thee die, beyond the tomb
Thy light shall shine: as sunk beneath the West
Though the great Summer Sun eludes our gaze,
Still burns wide Heaven with his distended blaze.[13]

---

13.   This was the first of a series of poems by Coleridge in the *Morning Chronicle* from December 1, 1794 to January 29, 1795. The "Eminent Contempories" to whom the poet addressed them included Burke, La Fayette, Pitt and Sheridan.

Select Bibliography

A. *British Museum. Additional Mss.*
Erskine Correspondence:
29,169: 29,475: 35,648: 35,649: 39,873: 44,992: 45,880.

Francis Place Papers:
35,154.

B. *Reports and Collections*
Criminal Statistics. Cmnd. 7670.
East Reports (Sir Edward Hyde East).
Parliamentary History. 1784. 1795.
Parliamentary Debates. 1804-10. 1818-19.
Hansard. 1820.

C. *Newspapers and Journals*
Annual Register 1788.
Edinburgh Review 1810.
Gentleman's Magazine 1853.
Law Society's Gazette 1994.
Morning Chronicle 1823.
The Times 1820. 1826.

D. *Books, Pamphlets and Articles*
Battersby, Celia. "Bench Marks". *Law Society's Gazette*. (1994).

Beccaria, Cesare. *Dei Delitti e delle Pene.* (1769).

Bentham, Jeremy. *Works* 11 vols. (1843).

Boswell, James. *Life of Johnson.* (1799).

Brougham, Lord Henry. *Historical Sketches of Statesmen who Flourished in the Time of George III.* (1839).

Buckle, Henry. *History of Civilization in England.* 2 vols. (1924).

Campbell, Lord John. *Lives of the Chancellors.* vi. (1847). Campbell's *Lives* are not uniformly reliable but he knew Erskine and had a deep regard for him.

Carey, John. *The Faber Book of Reportage.* (1987).

Churchill, Charles. *Rosciad.* (1761).

Cockburn, Lord. *Examination of the Trials of Sedition ... in Scotland.* (1888).

Coke, Sir Edward. *3rd Institute.* (1644).

Coleridge, Samuel Taylor. *Poetical Works.* (1924).

Creevey, Thomas. *Papers.* (c.1800).

Croly, Rev. George. *Life of George IV.* (1830). *The Personal History of His Late Majesty George IV.* 2 vols. (1841).

Dictionary of National Biography.

Ehrman, John. *The Younger Pitt.* (1969).

Erskine, Thomas. (Lord). *Armata.* (1825). *A View of the Causes and Consequences of the Present War with France.* (1797). *Speech on Animal Rights.* (1809). *Defence of the Whigs.* (1819).

Foss, Edward. *The Judges of England.* viii. (1864).

Green, J.R. *A Short History of the English People.*
(1874).

Hardy, Thomas. *Memoir.* (1832).
Holdsworth, Sir Wm. *A History of English Law.*
16 vols. (1903-66).
Holland, Sir Henry. *Recollections of Past Life.*
(1872).
Howell's State Trials. 1781-1820.

Lovat-Fraser, J.A. (MP). *Erskine.* (1932).

Macaulay, Thomas Babington. *A History of
England in the Eighteenth Century.* (1855).
Modern Orators. *Chatham, Sheridan, Erskine.*
(1845).
Montesquieu. *De l'esprit des lois.* (1748).

Nightingale, Joseph. *Memoirs of Queen Caroline.*
(c. 1820).

Paine, Thomas. *The Rights of Man.* (1792).
The Age of Reason. (1797).
Pellew, George. *Life of Lord Sidmouth.* (1847).
Phillips, Richard. *Erskine's House of Commons
Speech on Animal Rights.* (1809).

Ridgway, James. *Erskine's Speeches to Juries.*
(1810).
Romilly, Sir Samuel. *Memoirs.* 3 vols. (1840).
Roscoe, E.S. *The English Scene in the Eighteenth
Century.* (1912).
Roscoe, Henry. *Lives of Eminent British Lawyers.*
(1830).

Scarlett, P.C. *Memoirs of Lord Abinger.* (1877).
Stephen, J.F. (Sir). *Nuncomar and Impey.* (1885).
Stryker, L.P. *For the Defense. Thomas Erskine.* (1947). A boisterous but partial story of Erskine and his times.

Townsend, William. *Twelve Eminent Judges.* (1846)

Voltaire, F.M.A.de *Candide.* (1759).

Wakefield, Gilbert. *Reply to the Bishop of Llandaff.* (1798).
Walker, Nigel. *Crime and Insanity in England.* (1968).
Wharam, Alan. *The Treason Trials, 1794.* (1992) This fine account came to my notice only after the present book was written.
Wraxall, N.W. *Historical Memoirs of My Own Time.* (1815).

Index

TE refers to Thomas Erskine

241

Also by John Hostettler

Fighting for Justice
The History and Origins of Adversary Trial

This book shows how adversary trial evolved in England only in the 18th century. Its origins and significance have tended to go unrecognised by judges, lawyers, jurists and researchers until relatively modern times when conflict has become a key social issue.

2006 | 140 pages | Ebook ISBN 9781906534165
Paperback ISBN 9781904380290

The Criminal Jury Old and New
Jury Power from Early Times to the Present Day

A first-rate account of the criminal jury—from its beginnings to the present day. This book deals with all the great political and legal landmarks and shows how the jury developed from fragile beginnings into a key democratic institution capable of resisting monarchs, governments and sometimes plain law.

'Recommended to any new law student': *Internet Law Book Reviews*.
'Not only informative but uplifting': *Justice of the Peace*.

2004 | 168pp | Paperback ISBN 9781904380115 | Ebook ISBN 9781906534080

More titles and full details at WatersidePress.co.uk